Neighbours: 20 years of Ramsay Street

First published 2005 by News Custom Publishing

Publisher
James Weston

Managing Editor
Matthew Clayton

Editor
Finn Bradshaw

Art Director
Randall Smith

Senior Designer
Alice MacRae

Contributing Editor
Tony Johnston

Assistant Editor
Lorin Clarke

Sub Editor
James Harrison

Photography
Peter Bryant, Erin Slattery, Mark Taylor, Channel Ten archives,
HWT Library, Grundy archives

Circulation Manager
Margaret Lemac

Editorial Production Manager
Michael Brown

Print Manager
John Batten

Production Co-ordinator
Cathy Murray

Quality Control/Imaging Manager
Graham Patrick

Colour Separations
HWT Imaging

Printed by
Imago

Published by News Custom Publishing, a division of the Herald and
Weekly Times Pty Ltd, ABN 49 004 113 937, HWT Tower, 40 City Road
Southbank VIC 3006 Australia.

ISBN 1-876176-78-4

Thanks

Projects like this simply would not be possible without the generous
time and energy of many people. Special thanks to: Felicity Carr and
Katrina Ray from Fremantle Media, Steve Murphy and Jessica Stanley
from Grundy, Jan Russ (Grundy casting director), Ric Pellizzeri
(*Neighbours*' executive producer), Carole Harvey (production designer),
Linda Walker (line producer), Peter Dodds (producer), Peter Bryant,
Alan Shade, Stephanie Bansemer-Brown and Heather from Channel
Ten publicity.

Neighbours

20 Years of Ramsay Street

NEWS
CUSTOM
PUBLISHING

The 2005 cast (in costume after a stage performance) celebrate *Neighbours* being inducted into the Hall of Fame at the 2005 Logie Awards, Australian television's highest accolade. *Neighbours* is only the second television show to be inducted to the Logies Hall of Fame.

Contents

An aerial shot of Australia's most famous
address: Ramsay Street, Erinsborough.

More than a serial

After 20 years of following the same, indefinable formula, Neighbours has become part of people's lives the world over. By Tony Johnston

Living with the same neighbours for 20 years is testament to a real community spirit. Some of the faces may change, but the dynamic remains the same and everyone, for the most part, stays happy.

In a real life suburb of any city, this would be an enviable existence.

As television shows go, the drama serial that is based in a Melbourne suburb, and goes by the rather quaint name of *Neighbours*, has lived up to those very same ideals. And it has made this serial, or "soap" as these shows are affectionately dubbed, the most envied product of its type anywhere in the world.

In 2005, *Neighbours*, made by Australian production company Grundy Television for its international parent FremantleMedia, chalked up an incredible 20 years of continuous production.

By way of recognition on its birthday year, the show was awarded one of Australian entertainment's highest accolades at the industry's night of nights, the Logie Awards. *Neighbours* was inducted into the Hall of Fame, making it only the second television program to be awarded this honour.

Yes, an unpretentious drama about the everyday lives of a group of neighbours and their kids in a quiet suburban cul-de-sac, has made the Australian lifestyle a template for paradise in nearly 60 countries around the globe, and reached a daily audience estimated at close to 120 million people at its peak.

In Australia it screens five nights a week on Network Ten, in Britain it screens twice a day, five days a week on the BBC. There are few places, apparently, where the easy-going Aussie lifestyle has no appeal.

More amazingly, perhaps, *Neighbours* is bigger in

OPPOSITE: The optimistic innocence of *Neighbours* is a key plank in its platform of success, as personified by Hannah Martin (Rebecca Ritters).

Britain than it is in Australia, with three million Brits tuning in daily for a slice of sunshine and easy-living. As you'll read in this book, many even save their cash and holiday in Australia to visit the real life Ramsay Street, the mythical home of the *Neighbours* mob.

The BBC's director of television Jana Bennett sums up the British phenomenon: "There's something about the humour and warmth of the characters, together with the great storytelling and the show's strong family values that appeals to an incredibly loyal UK audience ... plus that wonderful Australian weather also holds its appeal for all of us in rainy Britain."

Perhaps it's not surprising, then, that a small industry has evolved around (mostly) backpackers, from Britain and elsewhere, trekking to Melbourne in the hope of seeing the real houses of the fictional

Ramsay Street, and/or meeting some of the cast. As we discuss in the 'Street Party' chapter (page 156) an industry has emerged to cater to these devotes fans, providing tours, trivia nights and more.

Even the famous admit to being fans. Visiting British rock bands often demand to visit the *Neighbours* set. Tennis stars, opera singers, football players all want to shake hands and have their photo taken with a *Neighbours* cast member.

One disappointment for Formula One hot shot Ralf Schumacher when he visited Melbourne in early 2005, apart from not winning the Melbourne Grand Prix, was not having time to visit the *Neighbours* set.

Sounds crazy, doesn't it? But it's all true, and it further enhances the *Neighbours* legend.

The big question everyone asks is about the *Neighbours* formula for such enduring popularity and

FROM FAR LEFT: Holly Valance gets a visit from British Lions players Scott Murray (left) and Jeremy Davidson on set; Kylie Minogue poses with Australian Rules star Warwick Capper in 1986; rapper Mike Skinner with Patrick Harvey (left) and Ryan Moloney; Kylie with on and off-screen lover Jason Donovan.

success, and whether it can be bottled.

The show's Australian creator, Reg Watson, learnt his craft working in Britain in the early 1960s when *Coronation Street* and *Crossroads* were getting started, and used this background to devise a unique Australian drama formula.

But the UK components were largely bleak slices of British working-class life, and when Watson was commissioned by Australian TV producer Reg Grundy to come up with a serial for Australian TV, he chose to set it in middle-class suburbia, with sunny skies, a healthy infusion of young people and plenty of humour as well as conflict.

"The initial brief, was no more than to come up with a show that would rate," he says.

And rather than some secret formula, Watson says the storylines dictated everything.

"There were no hard-and-fast rules. It was to be about a group of diverse characters who lived next door to each other, and how they got along.

"Initially we had a happy family (the Robinsons), an interfering neighbour (the Ramsays), and a bachelor living with a stripper (Des and Daphne). The writers were encouraged to use stories that caused conflict, with neighbours having to take sides."

He uses the Charlene/Scott (Kylie Minogue and Jason Donovan) wedding, which still tops most fan lists of Most Popular *Neighbours* Moments, as a classic example of this set-up.

"With the Scott/Charlene romance and then wedding, each character in the show had a point of view. Some (including Jim Robinson) claimed it was stupid for a schoolboy to want to marry a girl just out of school. Others (Madge) thought it was romantic and

11

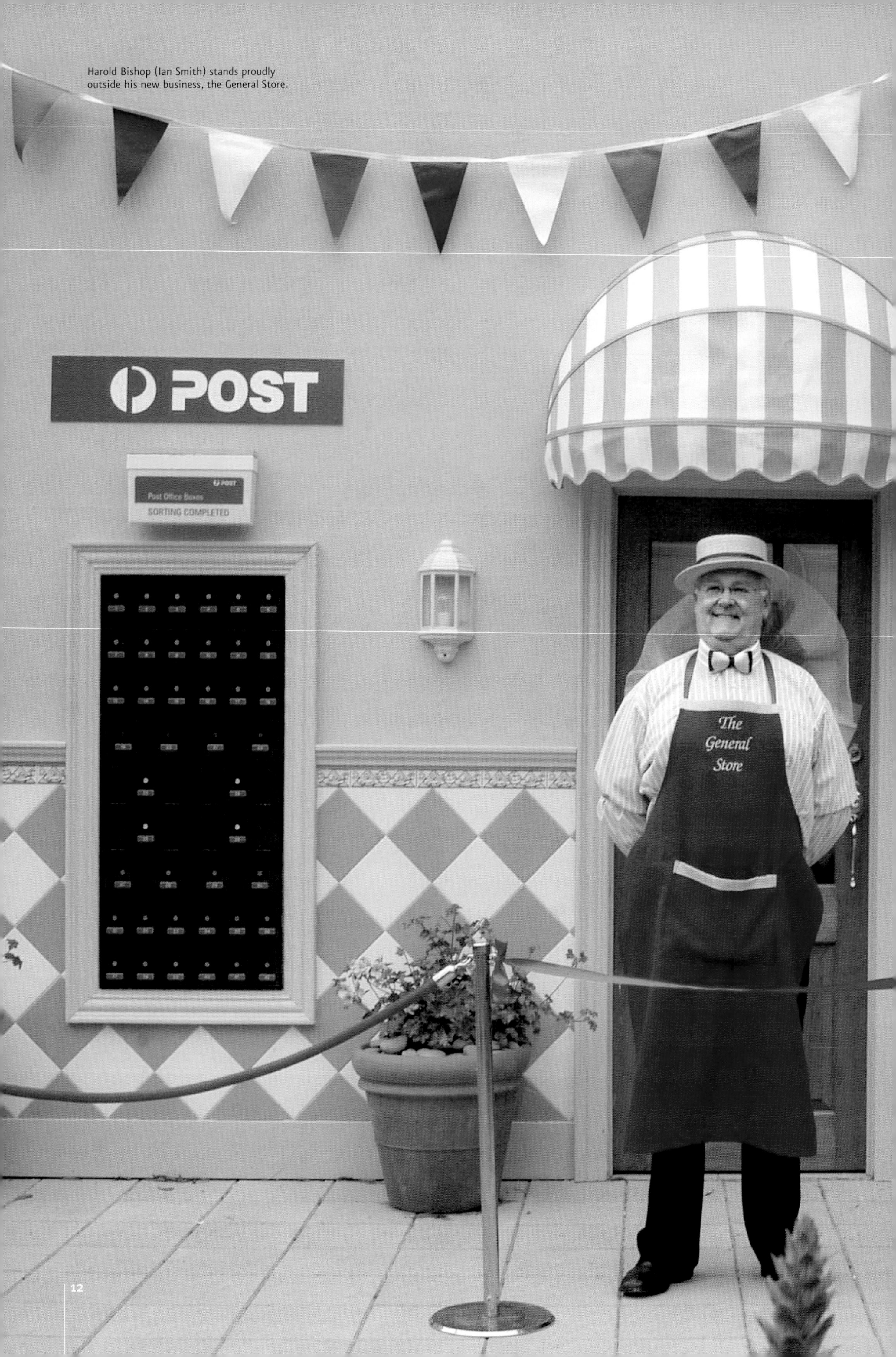

Harold Bishop (Ian Smith) stands proudly
outside his new business, the General Store.

POST

Post Office Boxes
SORTING COMPLETED

The
General
Store

BISHOP & CARPENTE[R]

GENERAL STORE

that the marriage would work. The story had repercussions for everyone in the street.

"It became bitter with Scott moving out, and so we eventually reconciled everyone for the high-rating wedding."

High-rating is an understatement. For the first time in Australia, at least, a fictional wedding for a TV show made the front pages of newspapers and magazines. Police had to be on hand to control crowds.

The succession of romantic entanglements that have been the backbone of *Neighbours'* plot lines are covered in great detail in 'Hunks, Babes and Romance' (page 28).

Of course, the flip side of these lighter plotlines are the moments of drama and intrigue. The *Neighbours* recipe depends on the show producing its fair share of

dramatic tiwts and turns, as remembered later in this book in 'Never a Dull Moment' (page 72).

It is testament to this "magic" formula, and the wonderful, insightful casting of *Neighbours* characters (in particular the young actors) that many of the show's actors went on to greater, even more illustrious careers (see the 'Brighter Lights' chapter on page 138).

It was no accident that Kylie and Jason went on to become superstars in their own right. Grundy's chief casting director, Jan Russ, who has chalked up 20 years on *Neighbours*, says even as young wannabe actors, Kylie and Jason had that something special.

She also goes to pains to point out that they, and many others that have gone on to bigger things, such as Guy Pearce, Craig McLachlan, Peter O'Brien, Radha

ABOVE FROM FAR LEFT: The wedding that stopped a nation; Scott and Charlene's nuptials even made the front page of *Time*; casting director Jan Russ; Rod Hardy, who directed the wedding episode.

Mitchell, Kimberley Davies and Natalie Imbruglia, didn't do so just on their looks and popularity.

"They all brought an incredibly professional attitude to their work. There were no prima donnas among them and in that sense they deserved to succeed," she says.

Even older actors, like Alan Dale (Jim Robinson), who now enjoys an excellent hard-won career in the US (with key roles in the likes of *The X-Files*, *The Practice*, *24*, *The West Wing* and *The OC*), look back on their time in *Neighbours* as not only career-changing, but life-defining.

Dale admits that when he was cast in 1985 he was desperate for work, with a young family to feed. "Getting the role in *Neighbours* saved my life and my acting career," he says now. "And looking back I feel a

great fondness for the show and the friends I made making it."

Actors haven't been the only ones to benefit from the *Neighbours* connection, and its almost workshop environment. Directors and producers who learned their craft on the "soap" are now spread widely through television and film in Australia and abroad.

Rod Hardy, who directed the famous Charlene/Scott wedding, these days commutes between Melbourne and Hollywood, where he has regularly directed on series such as *The Practice*, *The X-Files*, *The Hack*, *JAG* and *Battlestar Gallactica*.

"I look back on my days with *Neighbours* with great pride," he says. "The main thing I remember is that everyone – cast and crew – were so committed to making something special."

Another "graduate" of the *Neighbours* creative pool has been current *Neighbours* producer Peter Dodds, who started on the show in the early 1990s as a director. He is particularly proud of the camaraderie between cast and crew – "each week really is a collective effort" – and between younger and older actors.

Egos find it tough to find a toehold on the *Neighbours* set. It needs to be a collective effort; Dodds likes to use the analogy of the storylines being like a baton that is passed all the way along from writers to directors, crew and cast. The trick is not to drop it.

"The challenge (in the 20th year) is to keep it fresh and current," he says. "We are faced with the dilemma from the public, and the network as well, for

more stories with bigger and brighter characters. This means we are writing and shooting a third again as many scenes as we used to, but in the same amount of time.

"In 1985, we were shooting 12-14 scenes per episode; now it's 20 scenes, with more stories running through them. So *Neighbours* has become an exercise in time management and teamwork."

Despite this workload, Dodds says the production team is acutely aware of its responsibilities as well, not just to the viewing public, who have become far more sophisticated in their tastes, but to their own people, in particular the young actors serving their apprenticeships on the show. In a

sense, the success of those who have gone before them has raised the expectations of every young hopeful.

Dodds says a drama coach comes in to tutor the younger cast members. "They have also had coaching in things such as sword-play, martial arts and theatre improvisation.

"We want them to be able to leave *Neighbours* with a greater feeling for what they've been involved with than simply having appeared in a soap. Hopefully they will look back (as many of the actors endorse in later chapters) and realise that this show helped them to make their careers."

All of this, however, does not answer the $60 million question: why has *Neighbours* endured for so long,

and how does it keep finding a new audience?

Reg Watson now looks at the show through the eyes of a distant, but proud father. He offers another clue. "The original concept was also based on good communication between teenagers and grown-ups. Other shows played on conflict between parents and kids due to a lack of communication."

Neighbours then, puts young people into the adult world and hears them, listens to them.

And after 20 years their message is still the same: give us a chance and we can be anything. That's a pretty good dream for young audiences anywhere in the world, and perhaps goes a long way to explaining the success of *Neighbours*. ●

OPPOSITE: The changing face of Neighbours: (Left) The cast from 1987; and (right) in 2005, with some old favourites, for the 20th anniversary episode.

A Star of a Show

That it's still relevant and pulling huge audiences after two decades makes Neighbours something special. By Robert Fidgeon

*R*ejected by one Australian network, dumped after a few months by another, only to be revived by a third to enjoy a 20-year run, which shows no sign of coming to an end.

It's the story of *Neighbours*, a yarn far better than anything contained on the pages of a soapie script. But the story of Australia's longest-running soap is the stuff of small-screen folklore. That 20 years down the track it continues to survive ever-changing viewer taste and still attract a healthy audience stamps it as a rare television jewel.

The launch of *Neighbours* on Channel 7 on March 18, 1985 and its dumping just months later due to interstate network rivalry before Network Ten threw it a lifeline in 1986, are documented elsewhere in this book.

But it's *Neighbours'* continued popularity overseas, in particular Britain, that makes it a true phenomenon.

In looking to examine the reasons behind its success in Britain, where it more than holds it own with local favourites *EastEnders* and *Coronation Street*, we sought, first, the opinions of the ultimate judges – *Neighbours'* UK fans.

After all, this was a show that was purchased by the BBC, not because of its quality, but because it was on the lookout for cheap TV product to help fill its new daytime schedule. No one at the time imagined it would captivate British viewers to the degree it did.

Launching in the UK on October 27, 1986, it was soon being watched by 16 million viewers, and for a time outrated both *Eastenders* and *Coronation Street*.

In 1988, *Neighbours* was pulling an extraordinary 20 million viewers in Britain, as Kylie Minogue and Jason Donovan's Charlene and Scott won fans the world over.

Those golden days may have gone, but today *Neighbours* still screens twice daily, five days a week to three million British viewers each day. To put that in perspective, *Eastenders* screens to about seven million.

There's no shortage of television experts both here and in England who have offered theories as to why *Neighbours* has succeeded in Britain: the seemingly

PREVIOUS PAGE: Henry Ramsay walks Charlene down the aisle; everyone's favourite lollypop man; Harold Bishop; Max and Steph's low-key wedding. **INSET:** The dreaded Paul Robinson.
OPPOSITE: Fans gather together with cast members for a group photo on the Neighbours trivia night. **BELOW:** A panoramic view of Lassiters lake.

endless sunshine, the relaxed way
of life enjoyed by Erinsborourgh's
young people.

But while the experts love to
espouse far loftier reasons, it may well
get down simply to the characters – and
some excellent casting.

Married Lancashire couple Ruth and Barry
Henderson are longtime *Neighbours* fans. Both
discovered the show as teenagers in the early 1990s.
Now 28, and married for two years, the pair's love affair
with the Aussie soap remains undiminished. However,
it's a love affair that has nothing to do with the
sun-drenched Aussie locations or relaxed way of life.

As two of the 15,000 tourists, mainly British
backpackers, who each year make the pilgrimage to
Vermont South in Melbourne, which serves as the
location for Ramsay Street, Ruth and Barry feel
Neighbours is superior to its English counterparts

"When
I signed on for
Neighbours, I thought
I'd be here for a year",
says Fletcher, who
recently signed with
the show through
to 2006.

largely because of its characters.
"While the characters, as
with all soaps, have their ups
and downs, the characters in
Neighbours have more warmth, and
generally seem more satisfied with
their lot," says Barry. "The people in
EastEnders seem such a sour group by comparison."

For Ruth, whose favourite current *Neighbours*
character is Sky Mangel (played by relative newcomer
Stephanie McIntosh), the residents of Ramsay Street are
generally more interesting.

"Sky is a good example. She has a number of facets
to her character," Ruth says. "There's also no doubt that
earlier characters, such as Kylie's Charlene, and Jason's
Scott were hugely popular with British viewers.

"When you look at how they have gone on to
maintain their popularity in England, despite not being
in the show for about 15 or more years, says it all."

The Ramsay Street tour is big business, with up to 300 fans visiting the location each week. Ruth Henderson obviously isn't alone in her appraisal of Kylie's place in millions of hearts worldwide.

At one stage cruelly dubbed the "singing budgie" Kylie has gone on to enjoy international superstardom. Her late-80s on-screen love interest, Jason Donovan, left the show and immediately enjoyed huge popularity on the British musical stage.

At present, Donovan, real-life step-brother of Stephanie McIntosh, is enjoying a career resurgence, with impressive work late last year on Australian television in the legal series *MDA* and the telemovie *Loot*, before returning to London to wow audiences on the stage in *Chitty Chitty Bang Bang*.

Step-sister Stephanie could well be heading down the same track. On the strength of her growing profile in Britain, the 19-year-old blonde actress recently flew to Los Angeles at the request of British record producers,

where she recorded a number of songs for her first album, to be released later this year.

Longtime *Neighbours* regular Ian Smith, who plays Harold Bishop, recalls touring Britain with the cast in the late 1980s, and fearing for his life when fans almost overturned their bus.

"We were treated like royalty, but it was pretty intense, and at times quite frightening," he says. "Kids would risk their lives chasing after our bus down Regent Street. We knew nothing like it in Australia, and for ordinary actors it was all quite overwhelming."

Jackie Cook, a senior lecturer in communications and cultural studies at the University of South Australia, sees its appeal in Britain having a lot to do with reinforcing the British view of Australia.

"They see Australia as sunnier, more relaxed, less socially divisive, with the characters living in much better conditions than their counterparts in

OPPOSITE: The Neighbours tour is now officially sanctioned by Grundy television. ABOVE: Sky Mangel (Stephanie McIntosh) is one of the show's most recent favourites. ABOVE RIGHT: Kylie Minogue and Jason Donovan chat to a famous fan, Princess Margaret, in 1988.

Coronation Street or *Eastenders*," she says.

The show was so popular after just two years on air in Britain, that, in 1988, a number of the cast flew to London to appear before the Royal Family in a Royal Variety Performance.

The Queen Mother and Princess Margaret were huge fans, but not Prince Charles at the time, it seems. On being presented to the Royal family after the Royal Variety Performance, Prince Charles asked Kylie what series she was in.

While *Neighbours* might not today have the audience in Britain it enjoyed in the late-80s/early-90s, it is still a solid revenue earner for tourism in Victoria.

Twice a day, a bus crowded with predominantly British fans swings into the tiny cul-de-sac in Vermont South, and the fans alight and go to work with their cameras.

Derek, 22, is a Manchester United fan, and proudly wearing the jumper to prove it.

"I was about 12 when I first watched the show," he says, surveying the familiar homes. "My mum's just as big a fan, and would have come out here with me, but she's crook.

"To me, the show just has a lot more positive feel

FROM FAR LEFT: Backpackers surround the *Neighbours* tour bus in Vermont South; devotees with the famous street sign; female fans surround Alan Fletcher's band.

than our soaps at home. I've saved for two years to visit this street. Mum's a Kylie fan. No one will replace her in mum's eyes. Me? I'm stuck on Holly Valance. God, she's a sort."

Grundy program sales manager, David Byak, knows where Derek is coming from. Characters in soaps, and their relationships, play a big part in a show finding renewed appeal in overseas markets.

"The characters and their popularity play a big part in the show's fluctuating fortunes," Byak says. "The Bahamas has just picked up *Neighbours* again from where the Martin family exit the show, and the Scully family comes in, with Holly Valance (who played Felicity Scully)." This meant the show jumped more than 2000 episodes in the Bahamas.

According to Byak, the Holly Valance/Daniel MacPherson love story was extremely popular.

"Their romance re-ignited the flame for *Neighbours* in about four or five overseas territories," he says.

The halcyon days when *Neighbours* screened in 60 overseas markets have gone. Today, the show is seen in 23 markets outside Australia, still impressive for a 20-year-old program – in particular one that was axed in

1985 by the Seven Network on the basis it did not have broad appeal.

That decision is particuarly flawed when you consider how popular the show has been in non-English speaking countries. Iceland has an hour of *Neighbours* each evening. In fact, Grundy have had to ask the station there to slow down and cut it back to half-an-hour a day so they don't overtake the current production schedule.

Grundy takes particular care in working out which episodes to provide to a new country. Byak chuckles as he recalls the first episode that he provided to the Women's Television Network in Canada. "It's a network with a mainly female audience, so I started them off with the Full Monty episode as I thought the women viewers would get a good laugh ... and they loved it!"

However, Britain remains *Neighbours* biggest overseas market, and most of the British fans who visit Vermont South, also attend the Elephant and Wheelbarrow Hotel to take part in *Neighbours* trivia nights in the seaside suburb of St Kilda.

For a cover charge, up to 250 fans, most of them female, drink beer, applaud the arrival of Toadie Rebecchi (Ryan Moloney), Isabelle Hoyland (Natalie

Neighbours cast and crew prepare for the next take during the filming of the 20th anniversary reunion episode, 'Friends for 20 Years'.

Bassingthwaighte), Stuart Parker (Blair McDonough), Doctor Karl Kennedy (Alan Fletcher), and Harold Bishop (Ian Smith), to name a few, get autographs and meet the stars.

"When I signed on for *Neighbours*, I thought I'd be here for a year," says Fletcher, who recently signed with the show through to 2006, his 12th year.

At 48, Fletcher has also been a regular visitor to Britain in his Christmas break to star in pantomimes. Thanks to his profile on *Neighbours*, he recently toured the UK with his band.

The performing engagement was significant enough for Fletcher's wife, Melbourne television newsreader Jennifer Hansen, to seek network permission to accompany her husband on the trip and play keyboards.

Neighbours producer Peter Dodds believes the show's success in Australia and Britain is due to the fact it "tapped into the suburban dream".

"The families chat, the characters are interesting, and the viewer can relate to the storylines," he says. "British viewers, I think, see Erinsborough as a suburb with nice houses, great weather, and as a place where people genuinely communicate."

Until recently, Alan Shade operated the successful English website erinsborough.com – regarded by many fans as "the *Neighbours* bible".

Shade's internet message forum had more than 10,000 members, most of them British, all clamouring for the latest news from their favourite show.

"Why Britain embraced *Neighbours* so warmly is hard to pin-point," Shade says. "It wasn't the first Aussie import we had seen, but nothing before or since has ever achieved the same status.

"Certainly it allowed British viewers to get away from the gritty realism of British soaps. You could tune into the sunny antics of the beautiful people of Ramsay Street, and drift away from the stresses of your everyday life. I think it gives Brits a taste of a community spirit they no longer share."

Shade's view is echoed by 21-year-old Blackpool backpacker Angus Head, on a two-week *Neighbours* pilrimage to Melbourne.

"Bloody *Eastenders* is such a damned downer," he says over a beer at The Elephant and Wheelbarrow. "I've been a fan of *Neighbours* for almost 10 years, and while I'll look at *Eastenders* from time to time, it bloody depresses me. Everyone and everything's so sodding miserable.

FROM FAR LEFT: Scott and Charlene cut the wedding cake in 1987; the BBC's *Neighbours* website prior to a recent redesign; "Good sort" Holly Valance during her last *Neighbours* episode; Daniel MacPherson stars in *The Bill* as PC Cameron Tait.

"You watch *Neighbours* and come away feeling pretty good."

In assessing the success of *Neighbours* overseas, it is important that the contribution of the show's creator, Reg Watson, is not be overlooked.

Watson cut his TV teeth working in Britain in the 1970s on the then popular soap *Crossroads*, which began as a daily serial late in 1964, four years after the launch of *Coronation Street*.

His experience working in British TV saw him return to Australia in the early 1980s, keen to pursue the idea of an Australian-based serial that would have appeal overseas, particularly in the UK.

Watson attributes the show's success here and in Britain to its "real people".

"The original concept of the show was based simply on communication between parents and teenagers," he says. "Other shows at the time seemed to work on the opposite premise – that kids couldn't communicate with dad, and dad couldn't communicate with his kids – which I thought, for the most part, wasn't the case."

For years, many of the cast have headed to Britain during the Christmas recess where thay can command up to $20,000-$30,000 a week appearing in pantomimes in places such as Manchester and Blackpool.

In *Neighbours*' glory days in Britain, higher-profiled cast members could earn up to $60,000 a week headlining Christmas pantos in and around London.

Daniel MacPherson, now back in Australia hosting *The X Factor*, earned big money on the pantomime circuit before landing a 12-month stint in the hit British drama *The Bill*.

"Without the exposure over there on *Neighbours*, none of that would have come my way," he says.

There's no doubt it was Craig McLachlan's role in *Neighbours* that introduced him to British audiences, paving the way for stage roles in *Grease* in London, along with a starring role in the successful British TV series *Bugs*.

Neighbours regular Mark Little has just returned to Australia after 10 years working in Britain, including hosting the popular morning TV show *The Big Breakfast*. The opportunities that opened for Little in England stemmed from his popularity and abilities displayed in *Neighbours*.

Kimberley Davies, who played out-there hairdresser Annalaise Hartman, confesses she owes a great deal to *Neighbours*.

"It was such a great learning experience for us all," she says. "It taught us so much – discipline, technique, generally what was required of you as an actor to assist in making a TV series. And, of course, it was the launching pad for so many of us."

David Byak points out the show still remains a powerful launching pad today.

"It showcased Delta (Goodrem) to a world audience, Holly (Valance) started with the show, landed a No.1 hit in the UK in 2002, with *Kiss Kiss*, and is now looking to establish an acting career in the US," he says.

But for the Australian cast members, the popularity of *Neighbours* among young British fans not only served to swell their bank accounts and launch careers.

Ian Smith recalls being in London in the late 1980s, appearing in a pantomime, when he was asked to assist a young fan who was in a coma. A videotape of Smith speaking was played at the girl's bedside, who immediately showed signs of life. Within 24 hours she was out of the coma and Smith was a hero.

The show also has attracted some powerful celebrity fans. Susie Quatro has visited the *Neighbours* set in Nunawading at least once while touring Australia.

British pop group Steps visited the Nunawading set in 2000, while Human Nature appeared on the show in November the same year. The Pet Shop Boys are huge fans, and along with visiting the set, also appeared on the show.

It is only fitting, however, that the last word for the reason behind *Neighbours*' success should come from the man whose company created the show.

Australian television industry legend and founder of the production company that bears his name, Reg Grundy insists most of the credit is due to

ABOVE FROM LEFT: Craig McLachlan stars in the stageshow *Grease* in 1998, a role he reprised in 2005; Actors Madeleine West, Blair McDonough, Ian Smith and Janet Andrewartha celebrate the 4000th episode; Clive James during his cameo as Ramsay Street's postman for a day in 1996; Sometimes the world comes to *Neighbours*: Nina Tucker (Delta Goodrem) with her Bollywood PA, played by Curtis Fernandez. RIGHT: Reg Grundy, who credits a great deal of *Neighbours*' success to its original creator Reg Watson. FAR RIGHT: Actors Ryan Moloney, Daniel MacPherson, Andrew Bibby and Carla Bonner with the band Steps.

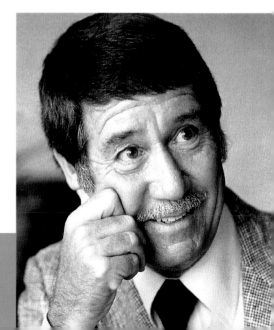

Reg Watson, the show's creator.

"In the mid-80s, when I sold *Neighbours* to the BBC, none of us could have foreseen what a milestone the show would become for British and Australian audiences," Grundy says. "At its height, *Neighbours* was seen in more than 60 countries, with a combined audience of more than 120 million.

"I wish one day Reg Watson will be truly recognised for his contribution to popular television drama.

"Amongst his many creations, *Neighbours* reigns as the longest-running series of them all. But like all good television programs, *Neighbours* is a cooperative effort.

"Every single one of the Grundy people who work, or have worked, on the show, deserve acknowledgement. *Neighbours* has always had that common touch, which crosses boundaries: hard to come up with, but involving viewing when it happens." ●

Did you know?

Your pantomime Neighbours include:
> Carla Bonner (Stephanie Hoyland) starred in *Cinderella*, as Cinderella.
> Mark Raffety (Darcy Tyler) played King Rat, in *Dick Wittington*.
> Anne Charleston (Madge Bishop) starred in *Jack and the Beanstalk*, as the Good Fairy.
> Dan Paris (Drew Kirk) was, unsurprisingly, Prince Charming in *Cinderella*.

Neighbours Rules Britannia By Alan Shade

For a show that developed a massive following, *Neighbours* made a surprisingly quiet debut into British television in October 1986. The BBC wanted a light serial that would appeal to housewives, and chose *Neighbours* from a crop of offerings that were mostly unrealistic US series that did not relate to the British public.

Neighbours was to be a daytime filler, nothing to get too excited about. How wrong the programmers were! Within months, it had become an obsession for students; school children were "bunking off" their lessons to catch it and word of its existence was spreading like a bushfire. The BBC soon caught on to the missed potential and, in 1988, moved it from the middle of the day to prime-time early evening. And there it has stayed.

In the 1980s, *Neighbours'* popularity was challenging those of hit British soaps *EastEnders* and *Coronation Street*. In 1988, recognising its huge impact, the cast were flown to London to appear at the Royal Variety Performance in front of the Queen Mother – they wowed the crowds by performing the show's famous theme tune live on stage. *Neighbours* had taken a firm grip on British society; another example of its unexpected success was when a newspaper decided to run a competition to win a trip to the set. It received more than a million entries and had to employ extra staff to cope!

Scott and Charlene's legendary romance captured the hearts of the nation, young and old alike, and their wedding went down in history as one the highest-rated episodes ever. No soap couple has ever quite matched their status in Britain and whatever Kylie and Jason have done since then, the British will never let them forget their Ramsay Street beginnings. For a time Kylie was one of Britain's most popular girl's names.

It is difficult to nail down why *Neighbours* has had such a huge impact on Britain over the years; it wasn't the first Aussie import, but neither before nor since has there been anything to match it. The gorgeous cast and the feel-good nature of the show certainly help – as do the pleasant, likeable characters. The perpetually sunny antics of middle-class Melbourne are a world away from the gritty realism of British soaps, so *Neighbours*

A newspaper ran a competition to win a trip to the set. It received more than a million entries and had to employ extra staff to cope.

32

proves a great escape from the stresses of British life and television!

Britons have good intentions to talk to their own neighbours and form strong communities, but it's far easier to watch people who already do it so successfully. The community spirit so evident in *Neighbours* is on the wane in Britain, so it's nice to see that somewhere in the world – whether it's a true picture or not – people still walk into each other's houses without thinking about knocking, take casseroles around to welcome new neighbours and band together in a crisis. Of which there are many.

Things have never been quite as good for the show as they were back in the early years, but it is still the BBC's most successful import ever and, despite changing viewing habits, it is still holding its own in the "soap wars". As the British soaps chase ratings with more episodes, more drama and bigger stunts – *Neighbours* could easily be eclipsed, but it is still consistently popular and loved.

Internet sites mean fans no longer have to wait months to learn what is going to happen in future episodes – now they can log on to *Neighbours* fan sites and get the latest gossip straight from Australia. Thousands of people from all over the world flock to *Neighbours* sites every day and fill discussion boards with opinion and speculation.

Every Christmas, *Neighbours* stars still take to the British stage – appearing as Peter Pan, Cinderella and a whole host of other pantomime characters. The response they get is massive, proving that *Neighbours* is still very much-loved in England; sceptical Australians need only pop along to a *Neighbours* backpacker night in Melbourne to see how mad the British fans still are for the likes of Harold, Doctor Karl and Toadie.

Neighbours continues to prove popular in Britain and, if anything, is on the up and up. Whatever the future holds, the impact *Neighbours* has had in England will never be forgotten and will almost certainly never be bettered. ●

Alan Shade formerly operated website erinsborough.com.

LEFT: Kylie Minogue meets Princess Margaret after the Royal Variety performance in 1988; **BELOW:** The 1988 cast on their trip to London to play to the Royal Family.

The 20 Most Memorable

Hundreds of characters have appeared in Ramsay Street since 1985. Here are 20 we have taken to our hearts — or loved to hate.

By Tony Johnston

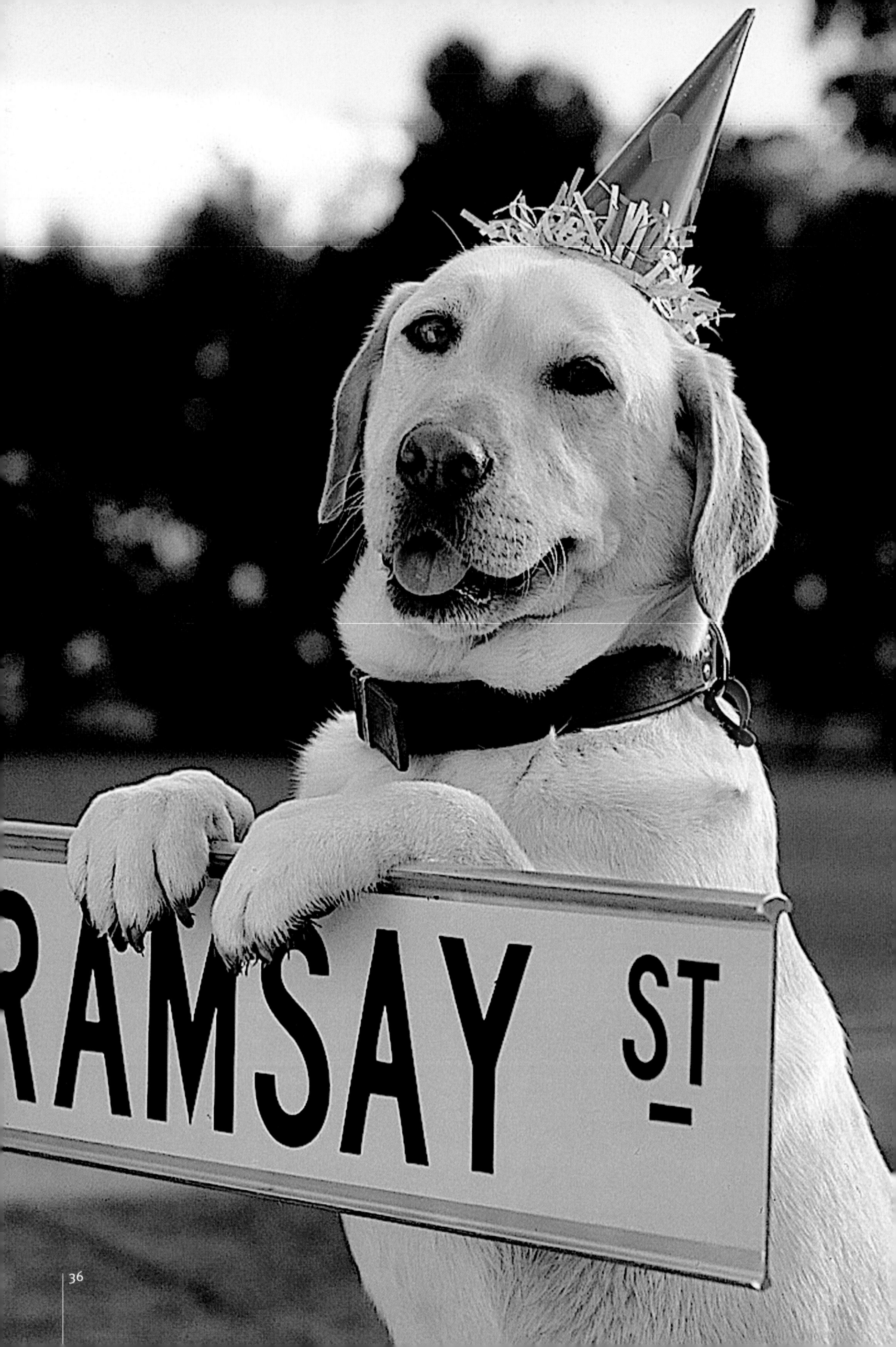
RAMSAY ST

20 Classic Characters
Over 20 Years
(in no particular order)

Honourable Mention

Bouncer

During his years in the show, Bouncer's fan cards were the most sought-after of any cast member.

He lived at three addresses – 26, 28 and 32 – but in reality belonged to all of Ramsay Street, and featured in many milestones for key characters, not least softening the heart of Mrs Mangel and saving baby Sky from a fire by barking down the phone for help. And, in true soapie fashion, he survived road accidents, being lost, a broken heart (over a bitch named Rosie), house fires, and even a nasty case of poisoning caused by some strange-looking mushrooms.

Mrs Mangel
Vivean Gray

She was only in *Neighbours* for two years, but the producers had Nell Mangel's part so well written and cast, that her shadow still looms over Ramsay Street, two decades on. Mrs Mangel, played by veteran actress Vivean Grey, was the Ramsay Street gossip, the Queen Bee of the cul-de-sac, and her constant interfering in the affairs of her neighbours did not always endear her to the street. Nonetheless, she was integral to the dramatic mix, with Grey reprising much the same role she had played earlier in the hit Australian period drama series *The Sullivans* (as Mrs Ida Jessop).

Mrs Mangel lived at No.32 and had a son, Joe (Mark Little), a loud and outgoing Aussie bloke who moved into his mother's house with his son Toby (Finn Greentree-Keane, then Ben Geurens), after his first marriage broke down. Mother and son where like chalk and cheese, but Mrs Mangel's ways were finally tempered when she met retired English dentist John Worthington (Brian James), and eventually left the street to marry him and live in Britain.

It is testament to Vivean Grey's performance that she imbued Mrs Mangel with such believability she was constantly accosted by outraged fans in public, many of whom found it difficult to separate the character from the actress. ●

1

Joe Mangel
Mark Little

The arrival of Joe Mangel in Ramsay Street added a new dimension to the life of the gossiping and interfering Mrs Mangel at No.32.

What initially amused locals and fans alike was how different the larrikin Aussie lad was to his mum.

The one thing Joe did have in common with his mother was the failure of his first marriage, which left him with a young son, Toby.

Joe took an immediate shine to Kerry (Linda Hartley), Harold's daughter, and when they married – romantically, in the Butterfly Enclosure at the zoo – he also became step-dad to Kerry's daughter Sky (initially Miranda Fryer, now Stephanie McIntosh).

But Kerry left the series in one of the more imaginative exits concocted by *Neighbours*' writers: she was accidentally shot dead while protesting against duck shooting season.

After Joe recovered (he found her body), he eventually found love again with the receptionist at Lassiter's Hotel, Melanie Pearson (Lucinda Cowden).

When Mark left Ramsay Street, he chanced his arm in Britain, where *Neighbours* had built an incredible following, and ended up hosting his own breakfast show on British TV. ●

2

Helen Daniels
Anne Haddy

Helen Daniels was the show's matriarch in the truest sense of the word for more than 12 years. Not only was she the linchpin of the Ramsay Street community, but she opened her heart and home to anyone in need of care and attention.

While Helen had a heart of gold – *Neighbours* creator Reg Watson has said he intended to break the stereotype of the interfering mother-in-law – it also often left her open to naïve personal judgments. She was married to her first husband, Bill, for more than 40 years and only discovered after his death that he'd had an affair with her best friend Grace. Other major tragedies included burying a daughter (and subsequently bringing up her grandchildren), and telling her other daughter that she was adopted. Helen married twice more, first to Bill's cousin Michael (who turned out to be a bigamist, causing the marriage to be annulled) and then to Rueben White, who died shortly after the wedding ceremony.

When Anne got seriously ill, her time off-screen was explained by Helen's own deteriorating health. She was in hospital (also off-screen) for some time before returning to the show to help settle the feud between the Bishop and Martin families. Soon after, Helen passed away quietly on the couch at home. ●

3

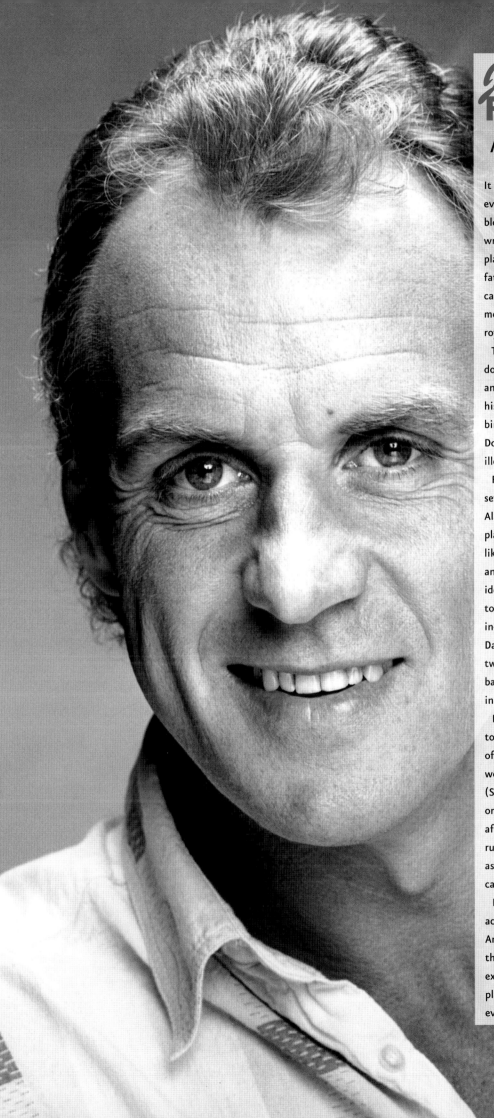

Jim Robinson
Alan Dale

It seemed Jim was related to everyone in Erinsborough, by either blood or marriage, and in a way the writers made it easier for him to play the often over-protective father, when they had him invent a car jack that earned him so much money he retired to live off the royalties. So he was always around.

There was nothing Jim wouldn't do for his kids – Paul, Julie, Scott and Lucy (especially Lucy, because his first wife Anne had died giving birth to her) ... and Glen Donnelly (his illegitimate son).

For more than seven years Alan Dale played Jim like a moral and idealistic son to his mother-in-law Helen Daniels, and the two of them were the backbone of the show in those early years.

Like Helen, Jim tended to fall for the wrong type of romantic partner: the final woman in his life, Fiona Hartman (Susanne Dudley), left him for dead on the lounge room floor of No.26 after he suffered a heart attack. She rushed to the bank to liquidate his assets. You can't get much more callous than that.

In contrast to his tragic soap life, actor Alan Dale moved to Los Angeles to try his luck after leaving the series, and has established an excellent new mid-life career playing strong character leads in everything from *Alias* to *The OC*. ●

4

Scott Robinson
Jason Donovan

Who would have thought that Helen's grandson and Jim Robinson's exuberant mullet-haired son Scott (initially played by Darius Perkins, then more famously by Jason Donovan) would become one of the show's most-loved characters?

Much of his appeal was that he played the sort of fly-by-the-seat-of-your-pants teenager that most teen viewers wished they could be.

He aspired to be a journalist, but Scott spent more time zipping around Erinsborough on his skateboard, finding other distractions and trying to grow up fast, rather than studying. He failed his final year of high school, but ended up getting a cadetship on the local newspaper.

More importantly, for most viewers, however, was Scott's wooing of Madge Bishop's daughter, the frizzy-haired young tomboy and mechanic Charlene (Kylie Minogue).

When the two married on the show, *Neighbours* gained its then best-ever ratings and Australia's newspapers covered the event like a royal wedding.

Jason and Kylie's popularity saw them move their careers into new directions, forcing the show's writers to ship the young couple off to Brisbane ... but they were careful to leave their back stories open. ●

5

Charlene Robinson
Kylie Minogue

Charlene was *Neighbours'* little girl with the big hair, the feisty tomboy daughter of Madge Bishop who, like her mum, was always determined to go her own way.

Charlene and her mum represented the old and the new, and they fought accordingly. If it wasn't over her clothes (overalls instead of dresses), it was over Scott. And her career work as a motor mechanic was certainly not a usual choice for young ladies.

And Charlene's razor-sharp tongue not only matched Madge at her best, it put the fear of God into all the Erinsborough boys who lusted after her.

No wonder she was instantly admired by girls everywhere … and loved by the boys for her feisty nature. Who could forget her whacking Scott one in the face the first time she met him? They were destined to be together.

Charlene and Scott were soapdom's Romeo and Juliet, and their marriage at a young age (in Australian TV's wedding of the year) gave hope to young lovers everywhere.

In 1988, at the height of her Charlene fame, Kylie set a still unmatched record by winning four Logies, including the Gold for Australia's favourite TV performer. ●

6

Madge Bishop
Anne Charleston

Madge arrived in Erinsborough like a tornado, not only livening up the bar at Lassiter's (first as a barmaid then as housekeeper and finally entertainment organiser), but quickly establishing herself as a woman not to be messed with. Her sharp tongue and neighbourhood feuds became legendary, making her romance and subsequent marriage to the mild-mannered Harold Bishop all the more extraordinary (and satisfying for true soap fans).

Madge and Harold's "odd couple" type bickering quickly became the staple comedy element for the series.

Despite this, it was no real surprise when Madge stood for the local council and was elected — who wouldn't want her representing their rights. Like her feisty daughter Charlene, Madge Bishop was a blessing in disguise for the Ramsay Street mob. Madge also reintroduced that biting tongue missing since the departure of Mrs Mangel.

When Harold went missing, believed dead, a heart-broken Madge moved from Erinsborough, the show lost its tragi-comic heart.

In the mid-90s, Harold miraculously reappeared. Soon after, Madge returned from her own exile.

Madge's death from cancer in 2001 was one of the most moving moments in the show's history. ●

7

Harold Bishop
Ian Smith

Harold loved Madge from his school days, when he competed with Lou Carpenter (Tom Oliver) for her affections. So when she turned up in Erinsborough in 1988, Harold was immediately on the hunt, and – after considerable competition from Lou – the couple were eventually married and lived at No.24.

Despite his initial fussy nature and comic edge, Harold was always a kind-hearted man, religious and full of integrity, which made him few, if any, enemies. So when he disappeared on the sea shore in 1991, leaving behind only his glasses, everyone assumed he was dead.

When he miraculously returned five years later, playing a tuba in a Salvation Army Band with no memory of his previous life, it was the highlight of *Neighbours'* often audacious 20 years of story-telling.

The new Harold was a milder man, as was Madge a milder woman, when they were reunited. But he still had his quirky traits, like an allergy to Bouncer's hair, and the ability to irritate the locals with his tuba-playing.

Erinsborough, however, wouldn't be the same without Harold, as he found out when he had his stroke and everyone rallied to his cause. These days, with Madge gone, the new "odd couple" is Harold and Lou ... but that's another story. ●

8

Lou Carpenter
Tom Oliver

Lou has been Harold's life-long friend and nemesis. They are the series' current odd couple, providing much of the regular comic banter, whether competing for the attention of the same woman or arguing over Lou's latest get-rich scheme.

Actor Tom Oliver has pulled off the remarkable task of imbuing a dodgy character with some irresistibly likeable qualities. Lou is a generally positive person, despite his failure rate, and jumps into each new challenge with enthusiasm. He is also loyal, and a ready confidant.

Lou arrived in Erinsborough in pursuit of Madge, and although he lost out to Harold, his love life blossomed even if his choices, like his business schemes, often back-fired.

Cheryl Stark (Caroline Gillmer) swept him off his feet (she bought every car in his car yard) and they had a beautiful girl, Louise (or Lolly). But when Cheryl was struck and killed by a car, Lou discovered he wasn't Lolly's real father.

Lou later ignored the attentions of Lyn Scully's mum Valda (Joan Sydney) and fell instead for Trixie Tucker (Wendy Stapleton). Trixie talked Lou into investing in a Hong Kong production of the musical *Hello Dolly*. When it flopped, Trixie took off and Lou lost all his money.

Still, Lou remains the eternal dreamer. ●

9

Annalise Hartman
Kimberley Davies

One of Lou's early dalliances was with the gorgeous and much younger Annalise Hartman, who took a job in the coffee shop, and pretty quickly took a shine to Lou, confounding everyone in Erinsborough (and in viewerland).

Was she just a gold-digger looking for a cosy lifestyle or did Annalise hold a genuine affection for Lou? Perhaps it was a bit of both. Either way, she spiced up the series.

Next she moved on to Mark Gottlieb (Bruce Samazan) only to be spectacularly dumped at the altar when he declared his love for Christ, and his intention of becoming a priest.

Next was the equally handsome young Sam Kratz (Richard Grieve); after a few hiccups she eventually followed him to Britain.

In her tragically brief, but spectacular run in *Neighbours*, Annalise set a benchmark of sorts by living in three different houses in Ramsey Street – No.24, 26 and 30.

Annalise returned once again to Ramsay Street in 2005 to present her documentary, much to the delight of the current young male residents. ●

10

Daphne Lawrence
Elaine Smith

The original owner of the coffee shop was Daphne Lawrence, who had spectacularly moved on from a career as a stripper.

One of the original characters in *Neighbours*, we first met Daphne when she was hired to strip at a Ramsay Street buck's night, and the wonderful Elaine Smith managed to imbue her with an appealing mix of cheek, savvy and the-girl-next-door. Here was a girl in charge of her own life, and she quickly became the series' first sweetheart.

One of the men at that initial buck's night was local bank manager Des Clarke (Paul Keane), and he was instantly smitten. It was not just lust in Des's case, he was genuinely fascinated by Daphne and pursued her despite competition from the then local hunk, Shane Ramsay (Peter O'Brien).

Daphne and Des eventually married, in *Neighbours'* first big wedding, and under her guidance the coffee shop became the local drop-in for troubled youngsters, who she would counsel.

Tragically, her own son Jamie would later be involved in a car crash that left his mother in a coma. ●

11

Shane Ramsay
Peter O'Brien

Shane was Max Ramsay's son, and despite the good looks and early-80s mullet, he was nothing like his domineering father. In fact, Shane was more of a quiet achiever, as he proved in his pursuit of Daphne.

As played by the charismatic Peter O'Brien (who has since gone on to become one of Australia's best actors and an international star in the making), Shane preceded Jason Donovan as the quintessential *Neighbours* hunk.

Older fans of the show will remember Shane's boxing match with Mike Young (another then-young hunk in Guy Pearce, now also an international star) over the affections of Jane Harris (Annie Jones). These three provided the original, and highly entertaining, love triangle of the series. ●

12

Izzy Hoyland
Natalie Bassingthwaighte

When Max Hoyland's little sister turned up in Erinsborough, no one had any idea how explosive her impact on the street would be.

Not only did Izzy attempt to come between Max and a very sick Steph, she also set about flirting with ... well, pretty much everyone.

It was her single-minded pursuit of Doctor Karl Kennedy that really threw the neighbours offside, and when she lied to Karl about her pregnancy – convincing him that he was the father of her child – it was very hard to sympathise with her. Izzy now finds herself alone, after Karl threw her out when he realised that she had lied to him about the baby.

But every now and then, it becomes clear that Izzy Hoyland is more than just a conniving, unscrupulous bad girl.

Serving coffees and gently ribbing her customers during her day job, Izzy is loads of fun, emotionally complicated, and often appears to feel genuine remorse ... although if Izzy teaches us anything, it is that appearances can be deceiving. ●

13

Paul Robinson
Stefan Dennis

Another character who took off overseas, only for vastly different reasons. One of the original Ramsay Street mob, Jim Robinson's son Paul (and brother to Scott, Julie and Lucy), recently returned to the show.

Paul was the show's resident ruthless, power-hungry wheeler-dealer for many years, although he didn't start out that way.

Originally an airline steward, then manager of Lassiter's, he was seduced by success and ended up running the Australian end of the Daniels Corporation.

There was nothing Paul wouldn't do for a buck, and at one stage famously planned to bulldoze Ramsay Street as part of a planned supermarket development.

Eventually, however, he overstepped the mark and was forced to flee to Rio to avoid fraud charges. ●

14

51

Henry Ramsay
Craig McLachlan

Arguably the leader of the mullet brigade, Henry was Madge's son and Charlene's big brother. And where Paul Robinson was a control freak, Henry was easily led ... which caused him to serve a prison term prior to his arrival in Erinsborough.

But, beneath it all, Henry was a happy-go-lucky bloke, with a ready smile and joke, and was always popular with the girls, although once he laid eyes on Bronwyn Davies (Rachel Friend) she proved to be the one for him.

Henry doubly endeared himself to *Neighbours'* fans when he came up with Charlene's dream wedding dress. He eventually found his calling as a radio announcer, and he and Bronwyn moved to New Zealand.

Craig McLachlan, who played Henry, is another of the *Neighbours* team who has gone on to a varied and impressive international career. ●

15

Jarrod "Toadie" Rebecchi
Ryan Moloney

If Henry Ramsay was the jokester of his era, Jarrod "Toadie" Rebecchi was the brunt of everyone's jokes when he first appeared on *Neighbours* with his "hillbilly" family: parents Angie and Kev and brothers Shane and Stonefish.

In the early days, Toadie looked set to follow in Paul Robinson's footsteps, or maybe Lou's – he was into any scam or money-making scheme going around. Plus, with those looks, we sort of expected he would have problems with the ladies.

But Toadie amazed everyone when he won a place studying law at university. The scheming jokester was suddenly taken seriously, and he began to mature into a sensible, and surprisingly ethical young man (he quit his job with a law firm after exposing a workmate's shady practices).

Even more surprisingly, after some early disasters with women, he eventually won the heart of his gorgeous flatmate Dee Bliss (Madeleine West), only to lose her when he drove the car off a cliff on their wedding day. Her body was never found (hint hint).

Still, Toadie to this day remains one of the show's most popular characters, representing the underdog made good. ●

16

Dr Karl Kennedy
Alan Fletcher

Doctor Karl is the pillar of the community, someone everyone can count on, and not just to look after their health. This has not precluded him from making his own mistakes.

Most notable of these were his role in the aftermath of the car accident that killed Lou's partner Cheryl, his dalliance with receptionist Sarah Beaumont (Nicola Charles), and his subsequent battle with the bottle when things didn't work out.

There has been his relationship with Izzy (Natalie Bassingthwaighte) and her claim that he was the father of the child she was carrying (the father was in fact Gus), leading Karl to do the right thing and take her under his wing. However, when he later found out the truth about Izzy and the baby, he was not so understanding.

Karl's sanity was even more sorely tested (not to mention that of his three kids Mal, Libby and Billy) when Susan slipped on some milk, hit her head and suffered amnesia that blotted out the previous 30 years of her life, including her wedding and marriage to Karl.

It was an audacious piece of plot-development from the writing team, and opened up an array of new story arcs, not least the stress of his love triangle with Izzy and Susan, which led to a heart attack (inset picture). ●

17

Susan Smith

Jackie Woodburne

From being the staid, occasional school-teaching mother of three (now grown) children, Susan has evolved into one of the show's most enigmatic and appealing characters, thanks largely to her bout of long-term memory loss, which effectively wiped out the previous 30 years.

When Susan's kids, Mal, Libby and Billy, left home, she initially tried to talk Karl into having another child, but when he freaked out, she turned to her teaching career.

Unfortunately, while she was teaching in the country to gain experience for a city posting, Karl strayed with his sexy receptionist Sarah (Nicola Charles). Then Susan had her outrageous accident … slipping on spilt milk and hitting her head.

But if the fans were confused by what followed (the writers had a field day), as Susan greeted everyone, including her children, as strangers, actress Jackie Woodburne obviously relished the challenge. And it showed in her performances.

Her achievements in *Neighbours* were recognised in 2005 with a nomination for Best Soap Performance at the prestigious Rose d'Or Awards in Switzerland. ●

18

Sarah Beaumont
Nicola Charles

The dark-featured and slinkily sexy Nicola Charles wasn't in *Neighbours* for very long, but she certainly left an enduring mark.

Until her arrival as his receptionist, Dr Karl had been a family-oriented, community-minded man. And although Sarah didn't need to make the first moves, she had a history of inappropriate choices in men.

She had arrived in Ramsay Street, moving into No.30 with her sister Catherine O'Brien (played by another star in the making, Radha Mitchell), to escape an ex-boyfriend in Britain who had turned into a nutter. (Both sisters obviously enjoyed a dalliance – Catherine was caught kissing Darren Stark when he was still with Libby). Sarah's fling with Karl wrecked his marriage, even though he ended the affair.

In many ways he is still seeking Susan's forgiveness.

Sarah eventually fell for a single doctor and they returned to Britain.

But even then, she couldn't quite let go, once famously sending Karl a truckload of manure (when she heard he was wooing Susan again), and on another occasion phoning him for a job reference. Gotta love her pluck! ●

19

Libby Kennedy
Kym Valentine

Actor Kym Valentine has had the unusual distinction of growing up before viewers' eyes on *Neighbours*, as one of Susan and Karl's three children. In her eight years on the show, her feisty character, Libby, has gone from blooming teenager to a married woman, mother and widow.

A headstrong and occasionally wild girl when she was younger – she had a long and rocky courtship with bad boy Darren Stark, and an affair with a university lecturer – Libby was nonetheless focused when it came to her career and general life goals. She eventually became a successful journalist (taking after Scott Robinson).

Her luck with men changed when she met the handsome Drew Kirk (Dan Paris), and they had a child, Ben. Even her unexpected labor and near death, in a barn at a rodeo, was pure soapie magic.

When Drew was tragically killed in a horse-riding accident, it took her some time to recover.

Libby returned to Erinsborough to be with her family, helping her mum through marriage problems before meeting up with a previous boyfriend, Darren Stark (Todd McDonald), and moving to Shepparton to be with him.

Kym left *Neighbours* to star as Baby Houseman in the stage musical version of *Dirty Dancing*, which became a big hit. ●

20

Hunks, babes and romance

Affairs of the heart have always been a staple of Ramsay Street.

By Kerrie Theobald and Tony Johnston

A key ingredient of *Neighbours*' enduring popularity has been its "hot young things", those cannily cast young actors who would become the soap's "hunks" and "babes".

Even in the show's 20th year, Grundy's senior casting director Jan Russ is still on a brief from the producers to find fresh and attractive young faces which will give the show a periodic burst of newness.

These injections fire up the writers, directors and the rest of the cast. They not only add freshness, but remind everyone that like in a real neighbourhood, people move on, new faces arrive and one generation cedes to the next.

There is the show's time slot to consider. In Australia, the UK and the more than 50 other countries that have bought *Neighbours*, the show is an anchor for early-evening family viewing. This means it must appeal to youngsters while amusing their parents.

One of the keys to *Neighbours*' universal appeal is that its characters share the same hopes and dreams that their viewers do, albeit often in a short time frame.

Another of its strong points has the been the appeal, both in terms of personality as well as physically, of its actors.

For the girls (who make up the majority of the *Neighbours* viewer demographic) there has been an endless stream of young, handsome, often cheeky, and quintessentially Aussie guys. When Jason Donovan took over the role of Scott Robinson from Darius Perkins, the tradition truly took hold. Then young rascal Craig McLachlan turned up, joining the list of *Neighbours* hunks: Peter O'Brien, Guy Pearce, Scott Michaelson, Daniel MacPherson, Dan Paris, Jesse Spencer, Jay Bunyan, Blair McDonough and many others.

If mums in the audience found some of these guys a bit too young, Alan Dale, Terence Donovan, Stefan Dennis, Ian Rawlings, Alan Fletcher, to name a few,

PREVIOUS PAGE: Paul Robinson and Christina Alessi share their first kiss. INSET: Ramsay Street darlings Scott and Charlene on their wedding day.

OPPOSITE: Scott and Charlene's wedding, perhaps the most famous television wedding of our time. BELOW LEFT: The original Scott Robinson, Darius Perkins. The role went to Jason Donovan when the show moved from Channel Seven to Channel Ten. BELOW: Latterday heartthrob Blair McDonough.

provided excitement for those who prefer a little snow on the roof of their heartthrobs.

The string of *Neighbours*' babes has been equally impressive, but the show's women also had to appeal to its army of young female viewers as well as to the male demographic.

The most famous babe, of course, was Charlene, played by latter-day pop diva and international superstar Kylie Minogue. Girls and guys loved her because she was headstrong, focused, cute, and cheeky. Parents even thought her not too bad a role model ... despite the hair!

Other babes who caught the public imagination were Daphne Lawrence (Elaine Smith, probably the very first), Jane Harris (Annie Jones), Gemma Ramsay (Beth Buchanan), Lucy Robinson (Melissa Bell), Bronwyn Davies (Rachel Friend), Annalise Hartman (Kimberley Davies), Anne Wilkinson (Brooke Satchwell), Beth Brennan (Natalie Imbruglia), Dee Bliss (Madeleine West), Gaby Willis (Rachel Blakely), Nina Tucker

ABOVE: Brad Willis and Beth Brennan, happy together at last. **BELOW FROM LEFT:** Men's magazine favourite Holly Valance; Kyal Marsh is sure to be one of the next generation's hunks; Des and Daphne's wedding; Henry Ramsay, always getting into scrapes, soon became one of the show's main heartthrobs.

(Delta Goodrem), Steph Scully (Carla Bonner) and Izzy Hoyland (Natalie Bassingthwaighte).

A clutch of others came and went after trying to upset the romantic applecart of those already listed, and a few married characters to boot.

Among this group were the likes of Sarah Beaumont (Nicola Charles), Tess Bell (Krista Vendy), Zoe Davis (Ally Fowler), Amy Greenwood (Jacinta Stapleton) Catherine O'Brien (Radha Mitchell) and Flick Scully (Holly Valance). But while they might not have been liked, they are certainly remembered.

Jan Russ admits there have been a few "misses" in casting potential hunks and babes down the years. But the successes have been legion.

Ultimately, the young actors and actresses who win roles on *Neighbours* have to then earn their fans. And when they do, it can be immensely rewarding.

Many of the standout sweethearts – Daphne, Scott, Charlene, Jane, Mike, Shane, Henry, Annalise, Sarah, Flick, Libby, Nina et al – are covered elsewhere in this book, so let's take a look at some of the other Ramsay Street legends; the parade of good-looking guys and gals that often hoisted new actors to the heights of fame.

Surfboard designer, and friend to all, Brad Willis (Scott Michaelson), was one such hunk. What girl could resist the charms of a blond, tanned surfer who matched his brawn with a caring attitude and a love of family? Brad Willis was quite a catch.

The girl who eventually caught Brad's eye was the sweet-natured and soulful Beth Brennan, who revealed a whole other (and for many young viewers, naughty and exciting) side when they were caught making love in the back of a van.

What also appealed about Beth, other than being Lucy Robinson's best friend, was her troubled past (there was talk of an abused childhood) and the way she went about reinventing herself, and finding her self esteem. Many young viewers could empathise with Beth.

One thing is for sure: with every great Neighbours romance, love didn't come easily.

ABOVE FROM LEFT: Joel Samuels got together with both Dee and Flick; Sarah Beaumont upset the applecart before finally marrying Dr Peter Hannay; Anne Wilkinson as the awkward teenager who blossomed into a strong, independent girl; Annalise Hartman and Sam Kratz became one of the hottest couples on Ramsay Street after Annalise was jilted at the alter by Mark; Nina Tucker and Jack Scully sharing a kiss.

Many of the boys of Erinsborough wished they could see more of Anne Wilkinson, who blossomed from awkward teenager to strong independent girl. Young Billy Kennedy saw more than most, however. The pair were caught skinny-dipping together, and it seemed to cement their bond.

Drew Kirk (Dan Paris) was the all-round nice guy every mother would love their daughter to bring home. Susan Kennedy was more than pleased when he teamed up with her daughter Libby (Kym Valentine) and they got hitched.

He came from rural Queensland – Oakey – and got a job as a mechanic in Lou Carpenter's (Tom Oliver) car garage. In his three years on the show Dan won his fair share of hearts among fans, who in 1999 voted him Sexiest Man on Television (*Inside Soap* magazine).

The gorgeous Dee Bliss, a nurse, gave every average Joe viewer hope when she eventually teamed up with housemate Toadie (Ryan Moloney), after dalliances with Joel, Darcy, and Stuart. In real life this beauty is also a stand-up comic, not to mention having graced many magazines.

Another favourite of the lads' magazines was young beauty Holly Valance (Felicity "Flick" Scully), despite the self-serving ways of her Ramsay Street alter ego, Flick Scully. Both Dee and Flick at one stage had eyes for the sporty Joel Samuels (Daniel MacPherson), as did many adoring fans.

But all that was in the past. Who are the current hunks and babes of *Neighbours*?

There's police officer Stuart Parker, (Blair McDonough) nicknamed "Chooka", who is dating Sindi. More famously, Blair (a *Big Brother* runner-up before being cast in *Neighbours*) and Delta Goodrem were a real-life item when she was in the series. Goodrem's character on *Neighbours*, Nina Tucker,

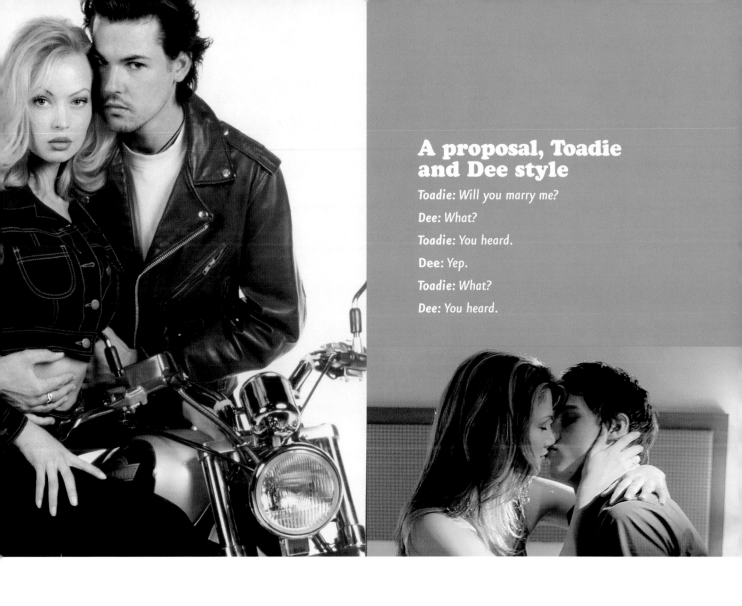

A proposal, Toadie and Dee style

Toadie: *Will you marry me?*

Dee: *What?*

Toadie: *You heard.*

Dee: *Yep.*

Toadie: *What?*

Dee: *You heard.*

found love with the much sought-after Jack Scully (Jay Bunyan).

And although she's sort of involved with Doctor Karl, Izzy Hoyland is definitely a babe. Her past speaks for itself – she was a Meter Maid on the Gold Coast! She is also funny ... and remains an inveterate flirt.

Young Boyd Hoyland (Kyal Marsh) looks certain to be the next generation hunk, although his first serious girlfriend Sky Mangel (Stephanie McIntosh), herself popular with young male viewers, dropped a bombshell on Boyd – that she had kissed another girl.

True to great drama formula, romance remains an essential ingredient in *Neighbours*. And the show has dished up its fair share of love stories and great couplings.

So far, there have been 25 weddings in 20 years. That's an average of at least one wedding a year,

although 1990, 1992, 1997 and 2000 passed without any Ramsay Street nuptials.

When we recall the great love stories in *Neighbours* we immediately think of the icons of the show – Scott and Charlene (see panel on page 67.)

One thing is for sure: with every great *Neighbours'* romance, love didn't come easily. There was always something or someone standing between the lovers, determined to keep them apart.

Before Scott and Charlene, there was Daphne Lawrence and Des Clarke, the stripper and the bank manager, who married in July 1986, cementing them as the first great romance, and still one of our favourites couples.

At first it seemed an impossible love triangle, with the handsome Shane Ramsay (Peter O'Brien) standing in the way. Ultimately Des's love, and sincerity, won Daphne's heart.

Steph and Max Hoyland marry in their own relaxed style.
From left: Lyn (Janet Andrewartha), Steph (Carla Bonner),
Max (Stephen Lovatt), Summer (Marisa Siketa) and Boyd
(Kyal Marsh) enjoy their new family.

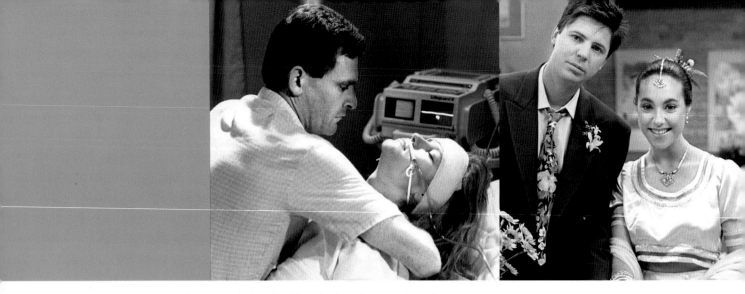

ABOVE FROM LEFT: Des clutches Daphne, the love of his life, as she dies in his arms in hospital; Joe Mangel and Kerry Bishop, the show's odd couple, married at the zoo; Scott and Charlene, the boy next door and the feisty blonde tomboy, with their wedding cake.

The tragedy was that what was turning into an enduring love was shattered by Daphne's fatal car accident.

A less immediately obvious coupling occurred between Paul Robinson and Gail Lewis, who were business partners in Lassisters. This highly ambitious pair initially considered love an unwanted distraction.

Their first marriage was purely business, but chemistry kicked in and Gail gradually fell in love with Paul. Thinking her love was unrequited, she planned to leave Erinsborough, but Scott Robinson played cupid and brought the two of them together again.

The ultimate golden couple is Harold and Madge. They had known each other since high school, in fact Harold had always loved Madge, but she chose to marry Fred Mitchell. When that marriage ended, Madge moved to Erinsborough, producing a lively rivalry between Harold and Lou.

It was Charlene who reunited the schoolyard sweethearts and, realising they were meant to be together, Harold proposed.

Despite the inevitable hiccups, they married and lived and loved for many years. Harold's disappearance in 1991 and reappearance four years later made their love affair one for the ages.

Kerry Bishop and Joe Mangel (Linda Hartley and Mark Little) married in September 1989 in the butterfly enclosure at the zoo. But then Kerry (Harold's daughter) was anything but conventional. They were an odd couple; Joe was a traditionalist while Kerry led a bohemian hippie lifestyle.

Stephen Gottlieb and Phoebe Bright (Lochie Daddo and Simone Robertson) married in January 1993, after a whirlwind romance. Phoebe was actually learning to love again after tragically losing her first love, Todd.

With the wedding imminent, Phoebe went into early labour, giving birth to a sickly premmie they named Hope (she was actually Todd's daughter).

Stephen married Phoebe in the marquee in the garden of No.22, receiving the ultimate wedding gift:

BELOW FROM LEFT: Paul Robinson and Gail, business partners and lovers; Harold and Madge, always happy together, packing the car for their trip to London; Madge finally marries Harold after more than a few hitches; Jason Donovan, straight from high school to media darling as one half of Scott and Charlene.

There's something about those two

Much has been written and much has been said about our all-time favourite couple, Kylie Minogue and Jason Donovan. They came to our attention as the loveable charismatic characters on *Neighbours*, fell in love both on and off screen, and went on to forge careers that continue to go from strength-to-strength on an international stage.

Funny, that in all the hype and publicity, particularly in the 1980s, not once did Kylie or Jason ever admit to being a couple in real life; they kept everyone guessing. Only after the relationship ended was it ever publicly discussed and then only briefly.

What was it that made these two so special, and helped put *Neighbours* on the map?

Neither Kylie nor Jason was new to acting, or working together, when they were magically cast as Scott and Charlene, but it was to be their first major, ongoing role. Both were straight out of high school, young, blonde and talented.

Their popularity was something that went beyond being in the right place at the right time. Kylie and Jason captured the hearts of the Australian public as no couple had done before. But it was a baptism of media fire as they became, almost overnight, international celebrities having to meet incessant demands for interviews, photographs and personal appearances. Even after leaving *Neighbours* their notoriety had a life of its own and the interest in their lives has never waned.

We have, quite literally, watched them grow up on the world stage. Both have achieved enormous success and both have had their share of lows. Their story is the stuff of fairytales.

It reads like this: Jason got the role in *Neighbours* just out of high

continued page 75

Hope was off the critical list and could come home.

As we mentioned earlier, Brad Willis and Beth Brennan provided one of *Neighbours'* more tumultuous romances. They were attracted to each other, but Brad was also attractive to every other woman (it seemed) in Erinsborough.

Their first attempt at getting married was called off by Beth when she caught a look between Brad and Lauren Carpenter (Sarah Vandenbergh), which turned out to be an accurate reading of the situation. However, Brad and Lauren's lust-filled affair quickly fizzled out.

When Beth and Brad finally did marry in December 1993, it was in the registry office, in an attempt to get away from their domineering parents. However, they later married again in the Robinson's living room to please the parents.

Mark Gottlieb and Annalise Hartman provided probably *Neighbours'* most bizarre romance to date. Annalise had initially set her sights on Lou, although most older locals thought that was a lifestyle choice rather than romance.

LEFT: Dee and Toadie at their wedding. The joy was soon to turn to tragedy. **BELOW, FROM TOP:** Phoebe and Stephen with Phoebe's daughter Hope; Libby and Drew share a kiss as husband and wife after the show's longest running courtship; Steph and Max, today's most popular couple. **INSET:** Kylie Minogue, whose career was launched in Ramsay Street.

The latter came with the handsome Mark, which delighted everyone. Unfortunately for Annalise, Mark dumped her at the altar in November 1994, after having a spiritual epiphany. He chose the priesthood instead.

Drew Kirk and Libby Kennedy's courtship was the longest-running in *Neighbours* history. They started off as good friends, although for Drew it was love at first sight. It took two proposals before Libby said yes.

But tragedy struck when Libby was involved in a motorbike accident. Told she would never have children, she called off the wedding. Drew finally won her back and the happy couple walked down the aisle in February 2001. Tragedy was to dog Libby, however, when Drew was later killed in a horse riding accident.

To most fans Karl and Susan Kennedy provide *Neighbours* most enduring romance. Despite the fact they are currently divorced, they obviously still care greatly for each other and many fans hope they will be eventually reunited.

They arrived in Erinsborough married with three children, who have since grown up on the show, before moving off to lead their own lives. They seemed to be a golden couple, although Karl has strayed several times.

Toadie Rebecchi and Dee Bliss had *Neighbours'* shortest marriage. This unexpected coupling – the beast and the beauty, so to speak – they started out as housemates before eventually falling for each other. But their happiest day ended in tragedy when Toadie drove their car off a cliff as they headed off on their honeymoon. Dee was never found, and is presumed dead.

Max Hoyland (Stephen Lovatt) and Stephanie Scully are the most popular contemporary couple, with a huge fan following. But the odds were stacked against them being a couple to begin with.

Max was a father of two whose wife had died suddenly. When Stephanie was diagnosed with cancer, she decided she couldn't put Max through the pain of possibly losing her as well, and walked away from love. He was left wondering why, until Stephanie finally told him the true reason. When he found out, it had the opposite effect, and they decided to cement their love.

Then, like 24 Ramsay Street couples before them, they declared their wedding vows in front of a worldwide audience of millions.

Which just goes to prove that if there is a moral to *Neighbours*, it would be that love will conquer all. Well, most of the time it will. ●

school. He then had an onscreen/off-screen relationship with Kylie, won a couple of Logies; made the leap from small screen to film. His duet with Kylie, *Especially for You*, went to No.1 around the world, including Britain, France and Greece. His album, *Ten Good Reasons*, was the highest-selling British album of 1989 and *Smash Hits* magazine voted him most fanciable man in Britain. He earned $100,000 a week playing Joseph, in *Joseph and the Amazing Technicolor Dreamcoat*. A proud family man, Jason won critical acclaim in the Australian telemovie *Loot* and the ABC series *MDA*. He is currently starring in *Chitty Chitty Bang Bang* in London.

Kylie won five Logies before she had left her teens, the youngest actress ever to do so. In 1987 the "impossible princess" released her first single, *Locomotion*, which became the biggest Australian single of the decade. Her debut album, *Kylie*, sold more than five million copies worldwide. Her first feature film, *The Delinquents*, was released in 1989, and since then she has starred with Jean Claude Van Damme in *Streetfighter* and as the green fairy in the mega-hit movie *Moulin Rouge*. Kylie has released an art book, a lingerie range, performed at the closing ceremony of the Sydney 2000 Olympic Games, had numerous sellout tours and won more awards than anyone can count. She has collaborated with some of the biggest names in the business. Her work with Stock, Aitken and Waterman, her duets with Nick Cave, Robbie Williams and of course, Jason Donovan, and her consistent record of No.1 hits have made her a phenomenon. She is only the second female artist (with Madonna) to have number-one hits in the 80s, 90s and "noughties". Kylie is truly one of the biggest names in music today. ●

Never a Dull Moment

From a lesbian kiss to who knows how many untimely deaths, Ramsay Street has seen it all. By Kerrie Theobald and Lorin Clarke

*E*very neighbourhood is full of characters, but Ramsay Street's characters seem to experience turbulence, life threatening illness and disaster on a scale unheard of in most suburban streets.

There have been many huge moments, but here's a look at some of the biggest shocks to hit our television screen over the past 20 years.

It's hard to believe now, but in the 1980s exploring teenage sexuality was still a shock to television viewers. Scott (Jason Donovan) and Charlene's (Kylie Minogue) Romeo and Juliet relationship was the original risqué *Neighbours* storyline.

Here were two teenagers openly expressing their sexuality in a show that wasn't about to shy away from issues like pre-marital sex. Watched like hawks by their parents, Scott and Charlene conspired to be together against all odds and despite staunch criticism from conservative busy-bodies like Mrs Mangel (Vivean Gray)

and even Harold Bishop (Ian Smith). When no one would let them move in together, the young lovers decided to marry. The audience loved it.

Almost 20 years later and the boundaries were still being pushed, this time with a lesbian kiss. We all knew that Sky (Stephanie McIntosh) was strong-willed and willing to try almost anything, but lesbian kisses are not yet a common sight on television. There were shockwaves when Sky locked lips with Lana (Bridget Neval). Vilified by ultra-conservative groups and celebrated by the gay press, the kiss helped to redefine *Neighbours* as it entered its third decade.

Infidelity is hardly new ground when it comes to television soaps, but no one saw this deceit coming. The married, committed, sensible and devoted Karl Kennedy (Alan Fletcher) stunned audiences when he kissed the young and sexy Sarah Beaumont (Nicola Charles) when comforting her after a break-up.

PREVIOUS PAGE: Lassiters explodes into smoke in the spectacular fire of 2004.
INSET: Libby kisses Drew as he is taken into hospital after falling from his horse.

OPPOSITE: Sky tells Boyd about her relationship with Lana. **FAR LEFT:** Lana's arrival stirred things up in Ramsay Street. **LEFT:** Boyd and Sky after being intimate for the first time. **ABOVE:** Scott and Charlene, with baby Jamie Clarke, had a relationship that shocked many viewers due to its open display of teenage sexuality. **ABOVE RIGHT:** Bridget Neval and Stephanie McIntosh, whose lesbian kiss shocked audiences in 2004.

Karl was the other half of the golden couple, the King and Queen of Ramsay Street. What was he thinking? Had he forgotten he was married to the dependable and lovely Susan (Jackie Woodburne)? Even on the day Sarah was set to remarry, Karl and Sarah kissed again, as he risked it all for a second time. For Karl, it was a fall from grace that continues to this day.

As the fall-out from his relationship with Izzy Hoyland (Natalie Bassingthwaighte) continues, sensible Susan gets on with her life, without him.

But, of course, in between her marriage break-up and her divorce, Susan herself had a romance ... with her Catholic priest. Vulnerable at the end of her marriage to Karl, Susan was looking for a firm friend who understood her.

Priest Tom Scully (Andrew Larkins) was a kind and caring confidante, but they grew too close and fell for each other. To make matters worse, Tom had rejected Lyn (Janet Andrewartha) in favour of a vow of celibacy many years before. Not only did Lyn entirely

ABOVE LEFT: Libby comforts Susan during her amnesia. **ABOVE RIGHT:** Susan Kennedy (Jackie Woodburne) and Catholic Priest Tom Scully (Andrew Larkins). **RIGHT:** Karl Kennedy and Sarah Beaumont enjoying an office relationship that was the beginning of the end for golden couple Susan and Karl.

Karl was the other half of the golden couple, the King and Queen of Ramsay Street. What was he thinking?

Did you know?

Causes of death on Ramsay Street include cancer, heart problems, shootings, car accidents, riding accidents, and in one case, tumbling from a tower on a murder mystery weekend.

disapprove, but the pressure the relationship put on Tom eventually drove him from Erinsborough.

Harold Bishop (Ian Smith) went from mumbling at customers and chastising people in the coffee shop to being at the epicentre of a gob-smacking drama in a single day. The affable Harold was washed out to sea in 1991, leaving behind only his glasses on the rocks. Everyone thought he was dead, including Madge (Anne Charleston). Madge left Erinsborough behind her after Harold was stolen away, but she

returned in highly unusual circumstances in 1996 to convince the amnesiac Salvation Army Officer who called himself "Ted" that he was really her husband Harold.

Harold's battle with amnesia and Madge's determination to reintroduce herself to the man she loved was both touching and funny, and the couple re-established themselves in the lives of their Ramsay Street neighbours.

Another case of amnesia shook things up on

Neighbours when, in 2002, Susan Kennedy slipped on some spilt milk.

Susan was diagnosed with retrograde amnesia, meaning that she didn't have any memories after the age of 16. Faced with living with a man she didn't know, and certainly didn't like, Susan struggled with her "new" life. She ran away to be with her high-school boyfriend, she had an overwhelming desire to go to Led Zeppelin concerts and she disliked her husband so much she instigated divorce proceedings. Eventually, Susan fell in love with Karl all over again, and they reaffirmed their vows.

In Ramsay Street, marriage certainly doesn't come with a guarantee of happiness. Early in the series, Paul Robinson's (Stefan Dennis) first wife Terry (Maxine Klibingaitis) shot him when he discovered that she had been responsible for killing a man and framing Daphne for the murder. In 2002, when the married Maggie Hancock (Sally Cooper) shared a kiss with Toadie (Ryan Moloney), Maggie's daughter accidentally exposed the truth to her whole family and the Hancocks moved away.

Keeping the family dramas below the surface doesn't

OPPOSITE BOTTOM: Susan attempts to comfort a distraught Toadie, as he realises Dee won't be coming back. **OPPOSITE TOP:** Dee and Toadie at a bridal fair. **ABOVE LEFT:** Izzy discovers she is pregnant to the wrong man. **ABOVE:** Cody, shot during a drug bust at 30 Ramsay Street.

tend to work on Ramsay Street. The difficult Julie (Julie Mullins) was drugged and almost drowned in the backyard spa by her stepson Michael.

Felicity Scully (Holly Valance) and sister Steph (Carla Bonner) failed to appreciate any sisterly bond when Steph experienced the ultimate heartbreak: being told by her husband-to-be, at the altar, that he was in love with her sister. During Steph's engagement to Marc Lambert (David Karakai), he fell in love with Flick, who had developed feelings for him before she knew who he was. When she realised, to her horror, he was the man her sister was in love with, she fought against her feelings, but was unable to break away from him. It went all the way to the altar: Steph said "I do", Marc said, "I can't, I'm in love with your sister."

If life on Ramsay Street can sometimes be tough, death can be spectacular. The death of a much-loved member of Ramsay Street is always a shock, but none more so than when patriarch and pillar of the show Jim Robinson (Alan Dale) died. There was one person who witnessed his heart attack, and could possibly have saved his life, but she stood by and did nothing.

The scheming opportunist Fiona Hartman (Suzanne Dudley) rushed away from the scene of Jim's death to transfer his money into her bank account. The bereft Ramsay Street residents were furious, but Hartman was nowhere to be found.

The greatest tragedy of recent times was the death of Dee (Madeleine West). She and Toadie (Ryan Moloney) had planned a gorgeous wedding. The celebration was perfect, but then Toadie and Dee were torn tragically apart. Driving into the sunset for their honeymoon, one lover's kiss caused Toadie to lose control of the car and drive off a cliff. We watched, heart in mouth, as Toadie struggled to the surface, desperately looking for his beloved. Her body was never found. This episode won an Australian Writers Guild award for Best Script in 2003.

Years before, during a drug bust, a stray bullet went through the window of No.30 Ramsay Street. Cody Willis (Peta Brady), one of the show's most popular characters, was shot and killed just when we thought things were working out for her. Cody's old flame, Todd Landers (Kristian Schmid), also met a grisly end, when trying to prevent his pregnant girlfriend Phoebe

The Lassiters fire takes hold and the roof falls in during one of the most dramatic episodes of *Neighbours* in recent times.

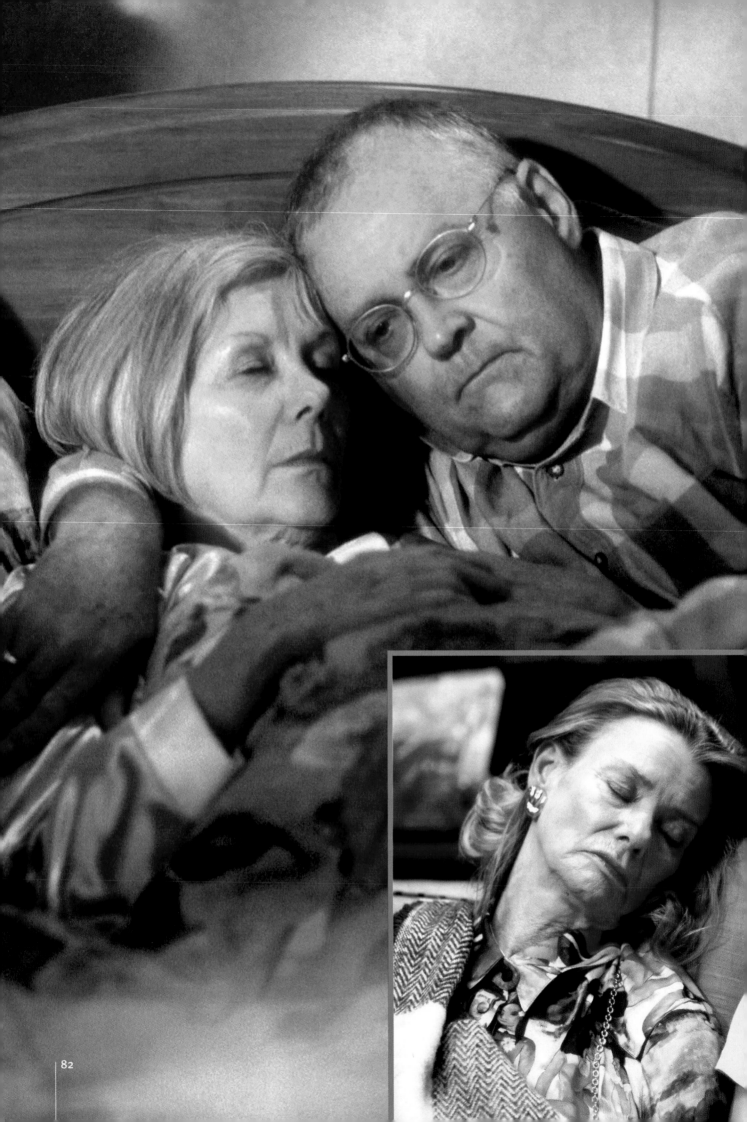

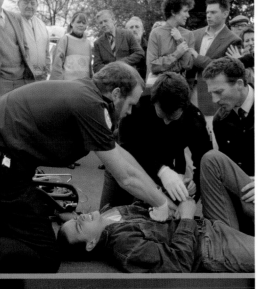

LEFT: Harold cradles the love of his life, Madge, as she dies in his arms. **BELOW TOP:** Todd's death was a huge shock. **BELOW LEFT:** Helen Daniels, with great granddaughter Hannah Martin, slips away in her Ramsay Street home.

(Simone Robertson) from having an abortion. Dashing across the road towards the clinic, Todd was struck by a car and later died, leaving Phoebe shocked and lonely.

In fact, it is usually the shocked, saddened and overwhelmed friends and neighbours of the deceased who are the most tragic figures in times of death. Lou Carpenter (Tom Oliver) was torn apart when the death of Cheryl in a roadside accident instantly made him a single father to baby Lolly, who was just 18-months-old.

And who will ever forget the effect of Daphne Lawrence's (Elaine Smith) death on her beloved Des Clarke (Paul Keane)? She was the first regular character to be killed on the show and her death changed Des' life forever. Shortly after giving birth to their son Jamie, Daphne was in a horrific car accident. She was in a coma for months and woke briefly to respond to Des' declarations of love, before passing away.

The only deathbed scene that comes close to matching that is Harold cradling a dying Madge in his arms. After enduring so much to be together, it seemed that nothing could tear Madge and Harold apart. But, sadly, Madge lost her battle with cancer just a few months after being diagnosed.

Libby Kennedy (Kym Valentine) was perhaps the most tragic case of those most recently bereaved. Drew (Dan Paris), finally back in his beloved Oakey and planning an exciting future, fell from a horse and was killed.

If there's beauty in death then Helen Daniels' (Anne Haddy) was serenely beautiful. One of the longest residents of Ramsay Street, her wisdom and acceptance were valued by young and old alike. Her death at home on the sofa, with her great granddaughter Hannah (Rebecca Ritters) by her side, was emotionally charged, even more so because viewers knew that in real life Anne Haddy was ill.

Not all tragedy on *Neighbours* comes from death. Lou Carpenter tore at our heartstrings as he fought for custody of Lolly. We watched in sadness as he discovered Cheryl had been unfaithful and that he wasn't the father of her six-year-old. Lolly's real father appeared on the scene and wanted to take her away. He did.

And to the baby we thought Libby would never have. After her accident in 2001, it was assumed she would never be able to bear children. That led her to calling off the wedding to Drew, but love overcame her doubts. They married and she did fall pregnant. While giving birth she flat-lined. It seemed she was going to die; we held our breaths until she pulled through and gave birth to Ben.

It was heartbreak at the altar for Mark Gottlieb (Bruce Samazan) and Annalise Hartman (Kimberly Davies). As they stood at the altar to say "I do", Mark looked at Jesus, looked at Annalise, back at Jesus and chose Jesus.

With death and disaster on Ramsay Street comes blame. Ramsay Street schemers and trouble-makers are nearly always suspected, and often responsible, for the most heinous of crimes. With the lines of good and evil blurred in the new-look *Neighbours*, there's a familiar schemer in town and we are only just beginning to find out what he is capable of.

FROM FAR LEFT: Jack Scully at his lowest ebb during his drug-taking period; Izzy makes it look like Darcy was trying to rob her; Steph realises the horrible truth at her wedding to Marc Lambert; the moment of truth for Annalise as she and Mark stand at the altar.

The ultimate heartbreak: Steph said "I do", Marc said "I can't, I'm in love with your sister."

Paul Robinson's return has hotted things up since he appeared in the crowd at the Lassiters fire. Not only has he reignited some old battles, but he has made new enemies very quickly.

Another schemer who continues to shock and delight audiences is Izzy. She spotted an opportunity to get what she wanted by lying to Karl Kennedy about her pregnancy, claiming her unborn child was his.

Her lie had enormous repercussions for the Kennedy family, driving a wedge between Karl and his children, while further infuriating the long-suffering Susan. Yet Izzy's deception continued; she was fed a dose of her own medicine when she was blackmailed by Darcy (Mark Raffety), before she framed him for robbery and left him in a coma.

In the land of soap the audience understands, indeed expects, that if a character does the wrong thing they will get their comeuppance. While *Neighbours* is not about to preach virtue, there are lessons characters learn as the drama unfolds. For instance:

➤ Honesty is the best policy. If Dee had employed it

and told Toadie she'd been married before, Darcy would not have been able to use the information to blackmail her and drive a wedge between her and Toadie.

> Don't drink to escape. Karl Kennedy hit the bottle once too often and came very close to being a full-fledged alcoholic. He was arrested for drink-driving, jeopardising all he had worked so hard for and hurting his family and friends.

> Never gamble more than you can lose. Doctor Darcy got himself in very deep with his gambling habits. Out of control, he stole from work and from his family and ended up in jail. Lance Wilkinson (Andrew Bibby) learned about gambling the hard way, too.

> Drugs are for mugs. Jack Scully (Jay Bunyan) had the world at his feet until his need to party saw him leap on the roller-coaster ride of drug taking. He put his health, his relationships, his family and his family's business on the line.

People don't learn lessons quickly or easily on *Neighbours*, though, and it's the sad, shocking, hilarious and rocky road to self-discovery that keeps us all watching, year after year. ●

Top five shocking goodbyes

1 Helen Daniels, on the couch with her beloved great granddaughter, passed away. "She's not asleep", said Hannah, starting to cry.

2 Daphne's last words, "I love you too, Clarkey" broke Des' heart as she slipped away.

3 When Todd died suddenly, leaving Phoebe pregnant and alone, she got to say goodbye when he appeared as a ghost in her mirror.

4 When Darren called Libby from a phone box to say goodbye, he left the receiver hanging limply beside an engagement ring while Libby called his name.

5 When Lolly's real parents came to take her away, she waved happily at Lou from the back window, as he held back tears and waved back.

Lucky Lucky Lucky

Kylie Minogue blazed the trail from soap opera to music, and plenty have followed. By Cameron Adams

Kylie Minogue

It could have all been so different. Kylie Minogue had flown from the *Neighbours* set to London to work with Stock Aitken Waterman (SAW), at the time the world's most successful pop producers. She'd had a No.1 hit in Australia, with a DIY cover of *Locomotion* – fuelled by her TV profile as *Neighbours*' overall-clad, perm-sporting mechanic Charlene Ramsay. Someone at Mushroom Records had seen Kylie singing the track at a Melbourne charity event and offered a one-off record contract. The song went on to become Australia's highest-selling single of 1987 and one of the biggest-selling singles in Australian history.

But the charms of Ramsay Street hadn't infiltrated the world of SAW, at least not yet.

So Kylie sat in a hotel waiting for a meeting with SAW. Days went by until someone reminded the songwriters (who'd had hits with Dead or Alive, Bananarama and Rick Astley) they had a girl from Australia wanting a song. Famously, they knocked off a jaunty little pop tune, *I Should Be So Lucky*, in the car on the way to meet her.

"I didn't know who she was," Mike Stock says in his book *The Hit Factory*. "I'd never heard of *Neighbours*. I sat her down for a coffee and asked her a few questions. In the end I thought, 'Well, she's 19, she's gorgeous-looking in a girl-next-door sort of a way, in the best soap opera in Australia earning huge money and she's got a great singing voice. You should be so lucky.' Then I made the move to, 'Well, she's got everything else in her life, but she hasn't got true love.' That's what the song is about. I wrote and recorded it in 40 minutes."

Kylie was out of there, on a plane back to Ramsay Street. The song sat in the SAW vaults for months until someone from the BBC started talking about the growing popularity of *Neighbours* among teenagers and Kylie Minogue's rising star. Mike Stock dusted off *I Should Be So Lucky* at a SAW Christmas party and watched it instantly fill the dance floor. They started shopping it around British record companies, who were equally unaware of the TV phenomenon about to kick in under their noses, and all of them passed on the song.

"They sneered at the idea because soap stars weren't appearing in the charts," Stock says. "Effectively, she was disdained by the record industry. You have to remember that even *Neighbours* itself was only on at lunchtime in those days. It actually moved to a peak slot when we had that hit, so nobody really knew her."

Fast forward two months. Stock Aitken Waterman

PREVIOUS PAGE: Kylie Minogue on stage at the Finsbury Park Mardi Gras concert in 2000. **INSET:** Jason Donovan, the second Ramsay Street heart throb to go to No.1 in Britain.

OPPOSITE: Minogue is ushered past fans and journalists in 1989. **LEFT:** Kylie's single *Locomotion* stayed at No.1 in Britain for six weeks. **FAR LEFT:** Kylie performs on stage, still sporting the Ramsay Street hairstyle. **ABOVE:** Kylie on the cover of her 1990 album *Rhythm of Love.*

ABOVE: Kylie and Robbie Williams, with whom she released the single *Kids* in 2000. MIDDLE: Two of the Kylie Minogue dolls released in 2004. RIGHT: Kylie opens her world tour 'Showgirl' in 2005. OPPOSITE: The *Ultimate Kylie* album, released in 2004. OPPOSITE RIGHT: Kylie and Jason, whose duet sold a million copies in Britain alone

released *I Should Be So Lucky* themselves. They pressed a few thousand copies to test the market and soon had orders for 800,000. Kylie Minogue had the spot No.1 in Britain (it stayed on top for six weeks, selling millions) and pop music had a new ally: the TV soap opera. It had happened before – most notably when *Eastenders* heartthrob Nick Berry hit No.1 in Britain in 1985 with *Every Loser Wins* – but most soap hits were one-off novelties; Kylie used a soap profile to launch a musical career.

Kylie Minogue may not have started the gravy train that took TV soap stars into the pop charts, but she got into the driver's seat and cranked up the engine. Her success changed everything; record companies realised that a huge profile on TV with the very demographic who buy pop records meant most of the work was already done – you just needed to get a record in the stores and let the rest follow.

And it did. Kylie Minogue became Stock Aitken Waterman's multi-platinum goose, churning out hit after hit.

But not without a lot of grovelling from SAW: Mike Stock flew to Australia after the success of *I Should Be So Lucky* to "crawl on my hands and knees" and apologise for making her wait. "By then I'd realised she was a star. She didn't have a big diva's voice, but it was immediately recognisable as Kylie Minogue. Kylie was very shy and didn't push herself, but when the camera went on her, she switched on and all the magic came out."

Stock even claims that the success of *I Should Be So Lucky* helped *Neighbours* become a massive hit show on British television, though he acknowledges the

show's large influence. "*Neighbours* broke the mould and every British teenager dreamed of becoming an Australian beach boy or girl," he said.

Stock says Minogue's *Neighbours* training helped SAW's infamous production line working methods, with albums recorded often in only a few days.

"Kylie was a trained performer and learned a script in a day for *Neighbours* so remembering a lyric was quite easy for her. Oddly enough, Matt (Aitken) didn't like (Kylie's) voice, he thought it was too tremulous. But as soon as you heard the voice, you recognised it. In the first few sessions I didn't want (Kylie) to have an input. I just wanted her to come in, sing and go, then we could get on with making the record when she wasn't there, because it was a bit embarrassing. She'd sit in the back crocheting socks and cardigans. After a full day on set, I'd get (Kylie) at night for two or three hours. The studio sessions were intense and it all got a bit too much for her. She was only 20 at the time and had been up most days since five in the morning.

(But) the real work went on behind the scenes. Matt and I were the backing band and they (the *Neighbours* stars) were the guest singers. I lost sleep and got grey hair trying to make them famous and keep their bank balances and egos inflated."

As her popularity outgrew the show, Kylie left *Neighbours*. But the hits kept on coming, and Kylie was growing tired of Stock Aitken Waterman's sausage-factory methods.

"I have no shame in admitting I was a puppet, but I didn't know anything about the business," Kylie remembers. "They weren't so interested in nurturing an

Kylie classics

artist, which was fair enough; that's the way they did things. It was literally 'Go make yourself a cup of tea; we'll call you when we're ready'."

Minogue recorded four albums with Stock Aitken Waterman in as many years, before leaving them in 1992. Her first post-Stock Aitken Waterman single, *Confide In Me*, steered her in a more credible direction. After pushing her artistic boundaries in the mid to late 1990s, Minogue returned to direct pop music in 2000, scoring her first British No.1 in a decade with *Spinning Around*.

In 2002, *Can't Get You Out of My Head* became Kylie's biggest selling single to date, eclipsing both *Especially For You* and *I Should Be So Lucky*, and returning her to the US Top 10.

She remains one of the most popular, and recognised, pop stars in the world and, after a period of disowning her *Neighbours* and Stock Aitken Waterman days, she's embraced her early output, perm and all.

This year, Charlene's overalls sat alongside her gold hotpants in a Melbourne exhibition of her costumes.

"I can see why artists resented my success in the early days," Kylie said in 1998.

"Suddenly this girl from *Neighbours* was releasing records and hogging the top position. They were releasing great music, while mine was doing very well. I have more respect than ever for Stock Aitken Waterman, because I realise how hard it is to come up with a No.1 hit, yet they churned them out consistently. They will go down in history and I'm proud to be able to say I was a part of that."

THIS PAGE: Jason Donovan on stage in 1995.
OPPOSITE LEFT: Donovan in 1995, the year he was in the paper more on account of his private life than his singing career.
OPPOSITE MIDDLE Donovan as Frank N Furter in *The Rocky Horror Picture Show* in 1999.
OPPOSITE RIGHT: Donovan as he appeared on Australian television show *Loot* in 2004.

Jason Donovan

When Kylie worked, it was only a matter of common – and financial – sense that her on-screen (and secretly off-screen) boyfriend Jason Donovan could work as a pop star as well. So, in 1988, Jason Donovan took the path Kylie had trodden a year earlier, flying to England to record with Stock Aitken Waterman.

One problem: Jason's voice. "As a singer he was not one of the best. He needed a lot of help," Mike Stock wrote in *The Hit Factory*.

Indeed, the production trio was initially hesitant to work with Donovan, thinking it wasn't right to work with both Kylie and Jason, but soon were convinced – by the bottom line. "Everyone was confident we could provide him with smash hits."

And they did. His first single, *Nothing Can Divide Us*, was a Rick Astley reject and a No.5 hit in Britain in September 1988. Then came people power: rumours spread of a Kylie and Jason duet. Stock Aitken Waterman not only didn't have one, they hadn't even thought of it, thinking the public might gag on the potentially cheesy concept.

One record store had 400,000 pre-orders for a Kylie and Jason duet that didn't even exist. When the producers found out that small fact, they sat down and wrote one: *Especially For You*. The title came from a Christmas card greeting (it was to be released at Christmas) and sold a million copies in Britain alone.

Donovan's next single, *Too Many Broken Hearts*, was recorded in a day and hit No.1 in Britain in March 1989. Stock flew to Melbourne again to write for Donovan's debut album, *Ten Good Reasons*, and also work with Kylie. However, Donovan (at the time a fan

of rock music) clashed with the producers when he wanted to "jam" in the studio; they had dozens more pop stars to get in and out of the hit factory. He told the producers his mates at the pub were teasing him over his pop tunes and he wanted to go more rock. SAW appeased him with the odd guitar solo.

After a second Stock Aitken Waterman album, Donovan left to star in a British production of *Joseph and the Technicolour Dreamcoat*, which spawned another British No.1, *Any Dream Will Do*.

Donovan famously sued a British magazine in the 1990s, after it questioned his sexuality, and became public enemy No.1 in cool circles. Later he collapsed in a nightclub, before admitting a problem with drugs.

"I didn't want to become the next Cliff Richard," Donovan said recently. "That's what a lot of people wanted me to do but it just wasn't my scene. I guess you could say I crashed the car."

These days are long behind him. Donovan has re-established himself as a well-regarded and successful actor. Two of his most recent appearances include the Australian medical drama *MDA* and the West End production of the stage show *Chitty Chitty Bang Bang*.

"I got into this to become an entertainer," Donovan says. "I'm proud of my past; it's made me what I am now, but I don't live my life through 1989. Yet those four years are always used as a benchmark."

He's also come to terms with forever being linked to Kylie. "It's going to be with me until the day I die. What she does is remarkable, I've the utmost respect for her but I can't escape her. It's such a long time ago, I'm amazed people are still so fascinated by that. It's irrelevant, really."

Delta Goodrem

No one has harnessed the power of *Neighbours* more than Delta Goodrem. Her debut single from 2001, *I Don't Care*, was released to little fanfare, finding its way into the wrong end of the Top 100 with few charmed by her Britney-esque pop.

Then someone in Delta HQ had a brainwave: seeing she was an actor as well as a singer, she could get a part in *Neighbours* as a character who could sing. She already had the record deal (with Sony); here was the perfect chance to launch her internationally.

Enter Nina Tucker, a shy girl next door with the voice of an angel. And enter Goodrem's change in musical direction. She'd tried to please her record company by going pop, now she would fall back on her love of piano balladry.

When *Neighbours* needed a song for Nina to perform in the show, rather than go with a cover version, Goodrem offered them a song she'd been working on called *Born to Try*.

Cleverly released to coincide with the song being aired on *Neighbours* as part of a storyline, *Born to Try* swiftly went to No.1 in Australia and went on to become one of the year's biggest-selling singles, going triple platinum.

"I could never have asked for that kind of exposure for myself or that song," Goodrem says. "It's not easy to launch as a solo artist. People can sit there and judge and say, 'Oh, she only got to No.60 with her first song, blah blah', but you know what? You try and break as a new artist. It's not easy. There are so many amazing acts out there. For *Neighbours* to ask me to be on the show, I was absolutely over the moon. It doesn't mean people are going to like it, you can get all the platform you like from being on *Neighbours* but if they don't like what they're seeing they're not going to go and buy it. But it was exciting to see how radio supported it and the people watching *Neighbours* supported it."

Goodrem has no problems with *Born to Try* being forever linked to Nina and *Neighbours*. "A good song will always stand on its own two legs, but at the same time you have to give it a bit of help. I can associate it with *Neighbours* all I want – it was on *Neighbours*, that's a fact; people first saw it on *Neighbours*. They took a gamble by putting this song on their show; it was the song I wanted on there, my song. And it was a beautiful partnership between myself and *Neighbours* and I think it caught a lot of people's imaginations.

"There's not even half-a-per-cent of me that would say, 'Oh, I didn't really come from *Neighbours*'. I feel completely happy embracing it; it's where I came from, it's what I did. I owe so much to *Neighbours*, I'll always be loyal to it. You should always be proud of the path you've gone on, being part of *Neighbours* is an absolute thrill and it's a brilliant time in my life."

Like Kylie and Jason before her, Delta continued to juggle filming *Neighbours* with the demands of a music career, flying to Britain when the *Born to Try* episodes aired there. She was rewarded with a No.3 UK single; her debut album *Innocent Eyes* sold more than a million copies in Britain and became one of only a

LEFT: Delta Goodrem, the gorgeous Nina Tucker, literally launched her music career on *Neighbours*.
MIDDLE: Goodrem was written out of the show when diagnosed with Hodgkin's disease.
RIGHT: Goodrem describes her time on *Neighbours* as "a brilliant time in my life".
OPPOSITE: Nina Tucker and Trixie (Wendy Stapleton) sing together on the show.

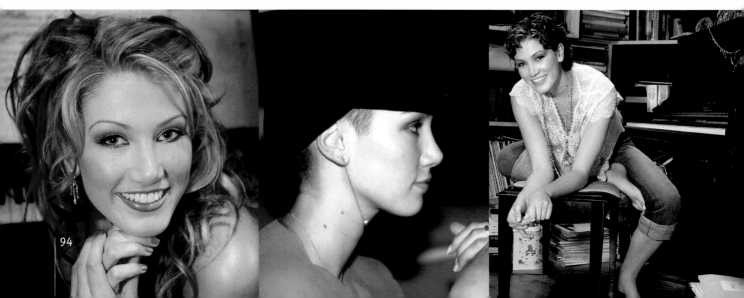

handful of albums to sell a million copies in the Australian market: one in 20 Australians owns a copy of her album.

The album was recorded during breaks in her *Neighbours* schedule during trips to Britain, then finished off in Melbourne with Goodrem often working in *Neighbours* during the day and recording all night.

"I was working every day and still doing music, it was the best time," she says. "I still have great memories of those nights."

Goodrem left *Neighbours* abruptly – she was diagnosed with Hodgkin's disease in 2003 – and Nina was written out of the show. When Goodrem regained her health she returned to film several episodes that tied up Nina's departure, and later filmed a cameo for the *Neighbours* 20th anniversary.

"When I think of Nina, I think about how I got to be a teenage girl and run around and do episodes where she was stuck in a bin, maybe do things that, because I wasn't at school, I didn't get to do as much. It was like leaving school and going into a school learning about something I really love. It gave me

a lot of responsibilities, too."

Goodrem's Australian chart record is nothing short of incredible: her five singles from *Innocent Eyes* all went to No.1 in Australia – something no other act has ever managed – while her second album, *Mistaken Identity*, has continued her multi-platinum sales, this time without the aid of being on a soap opera each night.

She's also the first to point out that unlike Kylie, she managed to pull off the soap-star-turns-singer role without any negativity.

"I have so much respect for Kylie, she went through hell. I guess when Kylie and Jason came out of the show into the charts it hadn't been going for quite so long so there wasn't that respect.

"But *Neighbours* deserves respect. When something has been around that long, it deserves that. Shows don't last that long in any country. It's a well-oiled machine that just goes and goes and keeps producing people, obviously there is something going on there, good discipline, it opens doors. What a show! You have to give it respect."

Holly Valance

Few were surprised when Holly Valance announced she, too, was going from Ramsay Street to the recording studio. She had the look, the profile and the "X factor". However, some suggested, she didn't have the voice.

Valance launched her musical career in spectacular fashion – covering a foreign hit, the Middle-Eastern tinged *Kiss Kiss*, which had been released by several artists around the world before Valance got her hands on it.

"I do like the ethnic side to *Kiss Kiss*, it's more interesting than doing what everyone else is doing, especially coming from *Neighbours*," Valance said at the time.

Memorably, Valance (who had posed in bikinis for men's magazines from the age of 15) appeared nude in the video, apart from some strategically placed lights and camera trickery.

"I was more concerned about making the break from the soap to this. It was a complete opposite direction because Felicity is a pretty little schoolgirl so we had to do something with a bit of shock factor and it's worked. Even though it's a bit raunchy."

wouldn't do it. I've had two sick days in three years and on both of those days I came to work and got sent home sick half way through. I'm happy being normal. I don't want everyone to leave a store I'm in or have my own changing room. If I go out I just want to fit in the crowd, I hang out behind my girlfriends and try to sink into the background. I don't understand demanding white lilies for a room you're in for an hour to do *Top of the Pops*. Who cares? Get in, do your thing and go home."

Valance's racy image and acting resumé saw her instantly compared to Kylie Minogue, who she ironically wound up competing with in the British charts.

"It doesn't bother me," Valance said. "She's wicked, she's fantastic; to be compared to her is a good thing. But I don't really see the comparison. We're both Aussie and did the same TV show – she did it 15 years ago – and we're both girls, but that's about it. We don't look alike, our music's not the same. I guess people have to write something."

Kiss Kiss went to No.1 in Australia and Britain in 2002, with Valance recording her debut album in both Melbourne and London, following the usual working methods of playing Flick Scully by day and recording by night. She soon left the series that made her famous.

At the time Valance, refreshingly down to earth for a pop star, impressed many by avoiding the kind of diva demands she could have legitimately pulled off.

"There's so many people relying on you, it'd be so rude not to turn up when you have 5am starts. I just

However, she did cross paths with Kylie once: when she was younger Kylie and Jason came into her father's shop. "They used to come in to my dad's shop and look around. I was really shy back then and they were the hottest thing on TV."

Valance's debut album *Footprints* spawned two more singles – *Down Boy* (written by Rob Davis, who wrote Kylie's *Can't Get You Out of My Head*) and *Naughty Girl* – but sold modestly, aside from being surprisingly big in Japan.

After an appearance at the ARIA Awards in 2002,

"I don't understand demanding white lillies for a room you're in for an hour to do Top of the Pops. Who cares? Get in, do your thing and go home".

FROM LEFT: Natalie Imbruglia in 2005; Imbruglia in 1997, having left *Neighbours*; Kylie and Imbruglia in 1998 at the Australian ARIA music awards; the hard-to-find *Christmas With Your Neighbours* album.

Valance moved to London after leaving *Neighbours*, where she recorded a second album, *State of Mind*, released late 2003.

After *State of Mind*, which did less well than *Footprints*, Valance moved to Los Angeles to concentrate on acting (apart from a cameo on an album by US singer Har Mar Superstar) where she's made appearnces in a movie (*House of Wax*) and on the hit TV show (*CSI Miami*) to add to *Neighbours* on her CV.

Natalie Imbruglia

As dorky Beth Brennan, Natalie Imbruglia captured viewers' hearts in Australia and Britain. Then after several years in the wilderness she came back with a new career – music – and won them all over again.

The success was simple. Her 1997 debut single *Torn* was a pop classic. Discovered by her record company after it was released to little fanfare by a band called Ednaswap, Imbruglia's version was an instant hit in Britain and Australia.

Imbruglia moved to Britain after leaving *Neighbours* in 1993, and spent several years looking to break into music. She admits those years were often tough, with her falling into the London party scene.

"The fact that I didn't work between *Neighbours* and singing sorted fame all out for me. I realised it was easy come easy go because people forgot who I was. I adjusted to being famous and then adjusted to the fact people have short memories. I think you always think you've bluffed your way there, but it gets more normal. I much more enjoy meeting people now than when I was working on TV; that was all about the character, which becomes impersonal after a while. It's nice to hear someone say, 'I like the words you wrote'; that's amazing.

"But my party girl days were quite a few years ago. When I first went to London I partied a lot. I dealt with that on my first album. (The song) *City* was about all the people I hung around with who I felt had bought me down, but it was my choice to hang out in that scene. I wrote about my wild days on the first album. It's so far behind me now."

Imbruglia's first album, *Left of the Middle*, was an instant hit, spawning four hits – *Torn*, *Big Mistake*, *Smoke* and *Wishing I Was There*. Imbruglia co-wrote much of the material, which was inspired by the angst-ridden guitar pop of Alanis Morissette.

She admits her TV history was crucial in crossing into music. "I still put getting my record deal, apart from having *Torn* on the demo, down to the fact I had the *Neighbours* profile. That was imperative. I don't know if I would have landed a deal as easily. I can't take anything away from *Neighbours*. I'm fully aware of what it did for me. I don't know how things would have gone without it. It got me out of the central coast (of NSW) and ended up

"I realised it was easy come easy go ... I adjusted to being famous and then adjusted to the fact people have short memories."
– Natalie Imbruglia

taking me to England; I'm forever grateful for the opportunity. But, at the end of the day, you still have to be good to have a career in music, but how great to have a door opened for you. So yeah, it got me in the door, but I think history shows (that) if you don't have the chops you get left by the wayside. But it's definitely a great launching pad."

Imbruglia says working on a daily soap was a perfect apprenticeship for the rigours of the pop business.

"Working in an adult world from a young age, it toughens you up. There was no one there to tell you to sign on and off so you get paid. Just basic things like that. It made me grow up really fast and, in that sense, it prepared me for the music industry. But I never see *Neighbours* any more. I don't think about *Neighbours* much. I'm glad I did it. But it's been a long time. I still get recognised from *Neighbours* all the time, especially in London. I get a giggle out of that."

And unlike most *Neighbours* stars, Imbruglia managed to score a hit in America: *Torn* was so popular in the US that *Left of the Middle* landed in the American top 10 in 1998, helping the album sell eight million copies around the globe. And in the US, no one had heard of *Neighbours*, meaning Imbruglia was judged solely on her music.

"That was nice. It was good to just be known for the music, have the song stand on its own two feet. That was a great feeling."

Imbruglia's second album, 2002's *White Lilies Island*, failed to match the sales of her debut, documenting a "black hole" in her life. Since then she's married

Silverchair singer Daniel Johns, who worked on her third album, 2005's *Counting Down the Days*.

Stefan Dennis

There was a joke going around in the late 1980s that even Bouncer might land a record deal and Stefan Dennis, who played Paul Robinson, is the first to admit that when he released a single some thought it was one musical crossover too far.

Dennis, who had actually had a long history in musicals and theatre, had first appeared on the hard-to-find *Christmas With Your Neighbours* album in the late 1980s.

He's refreshingly frank about what motivated him to release his debut single, 1989's seminal *Don't It Make You Feel Good*. "I mean, let's be 100 per cent honest about this: we all jumped on the bandwagon. There was the *Neighbours* phenomenon, then Kylie created the new phenomenon of spunky young actors being able to make a record. No offence to Kylie, she was in music long before she joined *Neighbours*. But the timing was right for everyone else."

Recording a voiceover for an advertisement, Dennis got talking to the studio engineer, who was also a musician. He asked if Dennis wanted to make a record. "I said 'yeah'," Dennis says. "It was that easy."

The original version of *Don't It Make You Feel Good* was in his beloved soft rock format. "If you find a copy of that, it's really rare," he says. "It didn't do anything!"

Then a remix was done in the UK, given a more uptempo feel. "That was the one that sold," Dennis recalls.

The single went top 20 in Britain (it didn't fare quite so well in Australia), with Dennis' video – in which he was draped in a leather jacket – still etched in people's memories. A second single, *This Love Affair*, was a chart disaster, missing the top 50 in Britain and not even charting in Australia.

"It was a much better song, but unfortunately me and that record were the meat in a political sandwich between the record company and the distributor; there was a war between them and the single got buried. And my recording career got buried at the same time."

Dennis says he can now look back and laugh at his attempt to capitalise on the Ramsay Street rock highway. "In retrospect I see it was my own stupid fault why my music career was so short-lived; I just didn't treat it seriously. The difference is Kylie did treat it very seriously, she had exactly the right people behind her – still does – and that's why she is the megastar she is. It was all a bit of a game to me. I should have been a bit more sensible. I took the songs seriously, but I didn't take the business side seriously. I was silly. I was having too much fun. But I'm able to sit back and take the piss out of myself now. I wasn't then."

Dennis and his musical partners had recorded a handful of songs for a proposed debut album before pulling the plug. "It's a shame, they're probably very dated now. They'd need a bit of remixing and tweaking. But if the right person came to me and said 'Would you want to make an album?' I wouldn't sneer at it. But I think I'm at an age now where it'd have to be 'Stefan Sings By The Fire'."

Craig McLachlan

When Craig McLachlan landed the job as larrikin Henry Ramsay in *Neighbours* in 1990, even he was shocked.

He was a muso biding his time working in a Sydney bar. "We had this communal staffroom," McLachlan recalls, "and we were about to start the shift. I was putting my foul, smoke-smelling vest on and my alcohol soaked, sweat-stained, stale-cigarette-odour bow tie and all the staff are crowded over this portable TV. I was asking for help with the ice, but they were all telling me to shut up because they were watching *Neighbours*. I was like '*Neighbours*? We have to do a double shift in this stinking hole, isn't life tough enough?'. The very next day my agent rang saying '(Grundy wants) you to audition for *Neighbours*, are you

RIGHT: Craig McLachlan and Guy Pearce in an on-screen *Neighbours* band, of which there have been many. **FAR RIGHT:** Craig McLachlan with his band, Check 1-2.

Did you know?

In 1998, when Toadie's job at the radio station was in jeopardy, he kidnapped Aussie singer/songwriter Dave Graney for an interview.

familiar with it?'. And I was like, 'As a matter of fact, I was watching it last night'. The rest is history. I mean, I'm an ex-plumber who played in crappy bands on the central coast of New South Wales. Nine months after unblocking my last toilet, I'm on the cover of *TV Week*. The only difference was I had the standard *Neighbours* mullet haircut on the *TV Week* cover, I wasn't wearing Stubbies and I wasn't covered in other people's excrement. "

McLachlan had a band before *Neighbours*, the Y Fronts, based in Sydney, that played the odd gig of all originals. He'd also had a covers band, playing songs like *Tie a Yellow Ribbon* at RSL clubs.

When he relocated to Melbourne for *Neighbours*, he started telling anyone who'd listen about his musical past – especially given the link between *Neighbours* and the charts. "While I was with the show, I saw the birth of Kylie Minogue: pop star. I remember hearing a demo of *Locomotion* in Jason's car, long before it was released."

Soon, McLachlan was thinking of reigniting his music career – with the help of Ramsay Street. "I think Stock Aitken Waterman even approached us … my feeling was that I would be third cab off the rank

and it'd die a death. At that point *Neighbours* was my first gig, I had no idea just how huge it'd be and how prolonged the success – particularly for some of us key cast members with the show during that crazy period – would be. I thought it'd be uncool to release music after Kylie and Jason."

Fate stepped in. McLachlan was asked to play a charity gig to raise money for cancer research; he flew the Y Fronts down to Melbourne for a show with no rehearsal. "I was shooting *Neighbours* during the day so we had no time (to rehearse). We bashed out two hours of material, probably every song we've ever played, and that was that. Over the next few days all I could think about was how much I missed playing with them. I wanted to call them and say, 'Let's get the band back together', to quote the Blues Brothers."

Soon McLachlan and the Y Fronts were playing a South Melbourne pub every week, packing it out and getting stellar reviews. "Ultimately, because of the success of Jason and Kylie and *Neighbours* reaching its zenith, major record labels started sniffing around," McLachlan recalls. "We sat around and went, 'Nah, we'll never play professionally again if we do anything

while I'm in *Neighbours*'. You were already hearing Kylie starting to be criticised on Melbourne radio, Jason certainly was, and I thought I could live without that.

"For years, the Kylie/Jason thing got worse and worse before it ever got better. Kylie was the 'singing budgie' for years, FM radio wouldn't play her music, Jason – forget about it. He wouldn't warrant a mention. But CBS came in with a deal that was, to use a classic showbiz cliché, too good to refuse. We thought if it was a pop record that was the band playing, we'd be OK."

CBS Records had a vision for the Y Fronts; they were quickly renamed Craig McLachlan and Check 1-2. Producer Garth Porter (of Australian 1970s band Sherbet) helped soften down the sound that had impressed audiences at the pub.

"The band was really naive. We'd never been in a big recording studio before. And the record was (nothing like) the live band's sound. People thought the record was wimpsville. Ironically, the record was successful, but the people who liked the live band didn't buy the record, or if they did, they gave it to their younger sister. A hit record was had, everyone was happy, but at the time I was shooting by day and laying guitar tracks down by night. We were being told, 'This will be a hit', and we didn't have the balls to say 'no'. I'm not whingeing, the album was a hit on both sides of the equator."

After the first single *Rock the Rock* was a hit, Porter heard McLachlan, a huge Kiss fan, playing Ace Frehley's solo hit *New York Groove*. He thought the chords sounded like Bo Diddley's *Mona* and suggested they do a remake. The song became the biggest-selling Australian single of 1990, and McLachlan's biggest British hit (it made No.2) – and his trademark song to date.

But the backlash to all things *Neighbours* had already kicked in. Commercial radio in Australia wouldn't touch *Mona*, McLachlan resorting to driving to local record stores to meet fans. And when he flew to Britain to promote *Mona* he found the knives were out.

"I had the credibility of playing the crappy, horrendous clubs – I can laugh about it now but we weren't laughing then – but it didn't matter. In England the backlash on Kylie and Jason was extreme and I just got caught up in it. While we were living it I was aware of the constant *Neighbours* stuff, but without wanting to sound like a wanker, at the end of the day, we could play our instruments. The disappointment came after you feel you've proved yourself as a good player that the crap didn't stop."

After the Check 1-2 album and follow-up hit *Amanda* (an original), McLachlan found his musical career in question. He went solo for a 1992 album *Hands Free*, a total flop record even he now laughs at.

"I went right off the deep end with *Hands Free*. If you listen to the guitar work it's like I'm simply focused on having to prove I can play more complex guitar solos and intricate chord inversions than any other guitarist on the planet. I'd forgotten about who bought *Mona*. When that album failed to sell in any way shape or form, I started to get called Craig McJovi. Then just as that album was about to be released Ratcat happened in Australia, three chords and snappy pop tunes and that signified the end of that late 80s/early 90s ultra glossy soft metal. I went '(Sod) it'."

These days McLachlan has a CV that includes everything from musical theatre (*Grease* in Britain and Australia), TV dramas and movies – and he has a new band, Mullet.

"It's like the more aggressive stuff of Green Day, it's cranked up." McLachlan says. "We'd get lynched if we didn't play *Mona*, so we play a fairly high octane version of it. The band's name comes from my old hairstyle. Actually, I just made it into a new hardcover coffee table book based on questionable hairdos, because of my physical athleticism they've called mine the Adonis Mullet!"

MAIN: The Blakeney sisters, or "The Twins", whose musical career came to a swift end in 1994. **OPPOSITE FROM LEFT:** Kylie Minogue during the "Showgirl" tour in 2005; Jason Donovan on stage; Delta Goodrem performs at the 2000 Sydney Olympics; Holly Valance poses for cameras in 2002; Natalie Imbruglia performs to Australian audiences in 2002; Craig McLachlan, armed with a guitar in 1998.

Gayle & Gillian Blakeney

Twins Gayle and Gillian had already had a minor musical hit in Australia with the 1979 hit *Singing in the 80s* – a novelty song released to mark the new decade. The girls, then in their teens, sang complete with Kiss-style makeup. After a stint in Australian kids TV show *Wombat*, they were hired on *Neighbours* as the Alessi twins, Caroline and Christina. Following the *Neighbours*-to-chart formula, they released a song with Stock Aitken Waterman as "The Twins" called *All Mixed Up* in 1991, which was one of the few Hit Factory flops. Two more singles, *Mad If Ya Don't* and *Wanna Be Your Lover* released in 1993 and 1994 respectively, helped bring their music career to a swift end. The latter hit the dizzy heights of No.65 in Britain. The twins have disappeared off the pop culture radar, they were last seen living in Los Angeles. ●

Neighbours

Four Months in the Making

From concept to screen, every episode of Neighbours goes through meticulous planning and a carefully choreographed production schedule. By Evonne Barry

NEIGHBOURS

SC 40

TAKE 6

EP: 4561

1

5

SHOT

DATE

1 2

On the scale of big *Neighbours* moments, the fire that devastated the coffee shop is up there with weddings and deaths.

The plywood eatery was Erinsborough's most famous landmark, a soapie icon established over almost two decades.

But the big bang of season 2004 that razed the coffee shop, along with Lou's pub and Dr Karl's surgery, was a milestone for more than one reason.

Never before in the 20 years of *Neighbours* had the crew attempted such an elaborate production.

The regular team became a cast of hundreds over five nights of filming, including up to 20 special-effects experts, the fire brigade and emergency services, triple the usual count of camera and lighting crew, and about 40 extras. Even the weather bureau was consulted, to ensure there would be no high winds and that conditions would be safe for lighting the fire.

And when the moment arrived, all looked to one man: Tony Osicka.

"We'd never done anything on this scale before," says the director of 19 years' experience.

"It was very much a case of being within the realms of television and biting off something you'd see in a feature film."

Despite all the careful planning and preparation, most daunting was the knowledge that the sets – real buildings in the studio's back yard – could be ignited only once.

"We had so many contingencies in place," Tony says. "There were so many different elements we had to look at because we were aware we only had one shot at it. Once it went up, that was it."

And go up, Erinsborough did. It burned for eight minutes before firefighters doused the flames and the three cameras stopped rolling. Only about two of those minutes made the episode's final cut.

PREVIOUS PAGE: Tom Oliver (Lou) prepares for filming on set.
PREVIOUS PAGE, INSET: Delta Goodrem has a laugh between takes.

OPPOSITE: The Neighbours clapper board for episode 4561, the episode where Nina (Delta Goodrem) returns to Ramsay Street.
ABOVE: The best footage is weaved together into an episode in the Neighbours editing suite. **ABOVE RIGHT:** Kym Valentine (Libby Kennedy) and Alan Fletcher (Libby's dad, Doctor Karl) enjoy Valentine's final day on set.

"It was a lot of work for very little screen time," Tony recalls. "But, then, that's usually the case."

Whether involving explosive drama or Ramsay Street small talk, all scenes go through the same meticulous preparation.

Every minute of *Neighbours* airtime – there have been more than 100,000 minutes over 20 years – is up to eight months in the creating.

It is, by necessity, a strict and streamlined operation, with more than 120 people working for 48 weeks of the year to produce 48 weeks' worth of the program.

Five episodes, collectively called "a block", are produced every week. But along the way, each block spends more than 30 weeks rotating through a tight timetable of planning, executing and improvising.

Script writing

A block of Neighbours begins life in the heads of seven people: two script producers and five storyliners.

Every Monday morning their ideas are morphed into a basic storyline, which provides a skeleton for five episodes. And each follows a specific formula; that is, it contains three "strands".

A-strands are the life-changing and emotional stories that keep people watching, like Charlene marrying Scott, Steph battling cancer, and Izzy lying to Karl about the father of her unborn baby. B-strands revolve around everyday romance; while C-strands are bits of light-hearted comedy that glue it all together.

"Every episode has to have an A-strand so there is a

OPPOSITE: The filming of the 2004 fire in the pub. **LEFT, INSET:** The planning of a *Neighbours* episode on the office whiteboard. **LEFT:** Linda Walker, line producer, with producer Peter Dodds in the background, during a busy day in the office. **ABOVE RIGHT:** Longtime script producer Luke Devenish with memorabillia.

reason for you to tune in every night, and then we work with a mix of Bs and Cs to keep it bubbling along and fun to watch," says script producer Ben Michael.

"What I really enjoy about *Neighbours* is that you will have an incredibly serious story rubbing up against a completely silly, funny bit of nonsense, mixed in with some romance."

After a week of storylining, the 20-odd scenes in each of the five episodes will have been detailed. Notes about the plot, the characters involved, and where the commercial breaks should fit in are sent to the producers, network executives and censors. Once approved, the scripts are sent to the writers, who spend a fortnight filling them out with dialogue.

And, finally, as the editors make their nips and tucks, all other departments begin making their own interpretations of the storyline.

Getting physical

Making the writers' ideas tangible is largely the job of the design department. Every prop seen in *Neighbours*, from the sets of every Ramsay Street residence to the teatowels Harold throws over his shoulder at work, is dreamt up, and either bought or made, by this team of 10.

"We are the first people that actually start making and producing something for the show, and we are the last people to walk away from it afterwards," says department head Carole Harvey.

The design crew gets about eight weeks notice to prepare for filming. When they learned the fate of the coffee shop, pub and surgery, Carole's team was told to replace them with a general store, bar and new surgery.

The construction and maintenance of regular sets in the main studio alone keeps two carpenters permanently employed. So the rebuilding of central Erinsborough (the Lassiter's complex exists on the grounds of Global Television Studios in Nunawading) was a monumental task.

All of *Neighbours'* facades, such as Izzy's ScarletBar,

have four solid walls, with a concrete slab, timber frame, and even electricity (so they can be illuminated from within for night scenes). The studio sets for all indoor shoots are built and bought from scratch, too, right down to the general store's foam profiteroles.

The responsibility of giving *Neighbours* its look also falls to the wardrobe department. The actors change in and out of almost 200 costumes over five episodes. In catering for that, wardrobe designer Peter O'Halloran oversees a team of five, and alone spends more than 20 hours a week shopping for clothes and accessories.

CLOCKWISE FROM BELOW: Carole Harvey, head of the Design Department, hard at work in her office; Ryan Moloney, Marisa Siketa and Patrick Harvey horsing around in a boxing scene; Peter O'Halloran, wardrobe designer, nestled among a range of costumes worn by the cast of *Neighbours*; Mark Raffety submits to a hair and makeup check by Natalie Stanley in the makeup room.

(The hotspots of *Neighbours* fashion are Chadstone Shopping Centre and Chapel and Brunswick streets in Melbourne).

Extras often wear their own clothes, but every time a new character is introduced to the show, the detail of their personality is expressed through their outfits.

"We have a little fashion parade in front of the producers and they might say they wanted the character to look a bit older, or more conservative, or a bit younger, than I had imagined," Peter says.

Developing a character, dealing with actors' weight gain or loss, as well as real and scripted pregnancies, are the wardrobe department's biggest challenges.

But the actors also have a say in their on-screen style. Or lack of it.

"I just don't want to send any of them in there to concentrate on 100 other things and feel uncomfortable," Peter says.

"But sometimes they need to. Sometimes it's scripted that Toadie (Ryan Moloney) is in a bikini, so that needs to happen."

The actors change in and out of almost 200 costumes over five episodes. Wardrobe designer Peter O'Halloran spends more than 20 hours a week shopping for clothes.

Props, lighting, costume, sound, and design elements come together during the filming of this scene in the pub, with actors waiting to enter, far left.

Did you know?

When developing the original concept for a television soap based in the Australian suburbs, executives and producers considered several potential names for the show. Eventually, they settled on the title Neighbours. Other contenders for the show's title were 'No Through Road', 'One Way Street', and 'The People Next Door'.

TOP: *Neighbours* producer, Peter Dodds. **ABOVE:** Actors Delta Goodrem, Ryan Moloney and Ian Smith relax away from the cameras. **LEFT:** Location manager, Mark Hancock.

Filming

A week before filming begins on a new block, all the involved departments prepare together.

Monday is reserved for directors, their assistants and the lighting crew to survey the shooting locations. All are found by location manager Mark Hancock, with the prerequisites stretching far beyond aesthetics. Council permits must be arranged, land and buildings hired, and dozens of people organised.

"You can't just turn up with the camera," Mark says. "You have to get the logistics in order. I call it 'the circus', because it virtually is."

The *Neighbours* caravan comprises at least three buses, for makeup and hair, wardrobe, and a greenroom, and eight trucks for props, equipment and catering. And that's just for a regular location shoot, and does not include the personal cars of cast and crew.

On the Tuesday of preparation week, focus returns to the script with everyone from the executive producer and production manager to the drama coach and casting director doing final fine-tuning.

On Wednesday, everyone involved in producing the episodes – this includes the directors, production manager, representatives from the wardrobe, art and props departments and lighting and audio teams, and those who monitor the program's continuity – get together.

A director's meeting follows, when the director and their assistants tinker with the details from all departments, such as last-minute changes to costumes.

Even the real-life residents of Ramsay Street – in Melbourne's Vermont South – are involved in this final week of preparation. They also receive copies of the shooting schedule, so they know when to move their cars out of their driveways, when not to be watering their famous gardens – and even when to expect extra attention from curious fans. One anonymous resident says: "They have pinched our letterboxes and they bring little jars along and fill them up with soil from our gardens."

But for the many months of meticulous planning, an actor's ill health, at any stage of the process, can throw the schedule into chaos. The most notable case was when Delta Goodrem was diagnosed with cancer and her character, Nina Tucker, simply disappeared.

"The last scene Nina was in, she was in the coffee shop and she was happy," explains Ben Michael. "And then, bang, that was it."

Aside from the emotional impact on the cast and crew, Nina's abrupt exit threw every level of pre-production into overdrive.

An actor's ill health can throw the schedule into chaos. "The last scene Nina [Delta Goodrem] was in, she was in the coffee shop and she was happy", explains Ben Michael. "And then bang, that was it".

Almost three months' scripts were reworked and a new character, Carmella Cammenitti (Natalie Blair), was introduced to fill the void.

On location

Five episodes of Neighbours are shot over two weeks. The first week is spent on location, filming outside broadcasts (OBs) and the second in the studio.

Line producer Linda Walker, who has worked on *Neighbours* for most of its life, says this schedule minimises the impact of weather, and other factors that are outside the crew's control.

"Bad weather is the bane of our life," Linda says. "But, luckily, it doesn't tend to rain in Melbourne for whole days at a time."

When it does, washed-out scenes can sometimes be shot in the studio a week later, with little impact on the script.

But more often, the cast and crew simply work through bad conditions. They have little choice, considering it takes a full day to shoot just six or seven minutes of screen time. And that's just for simple scenes, with few actors and basic props. Elaborate plots, such as the wedding of Toadie and Dee, and her subsequent drowning, are more difficult for all.

"We had to buy six suits for Toadie to wear to the wedding," says Peter from wardrobe. "They had to be a size bigger to disguise the fact he was wearing a wetsuit underneath. And we made all of his ties; we needed about 15 of them because he was in and out of the water."

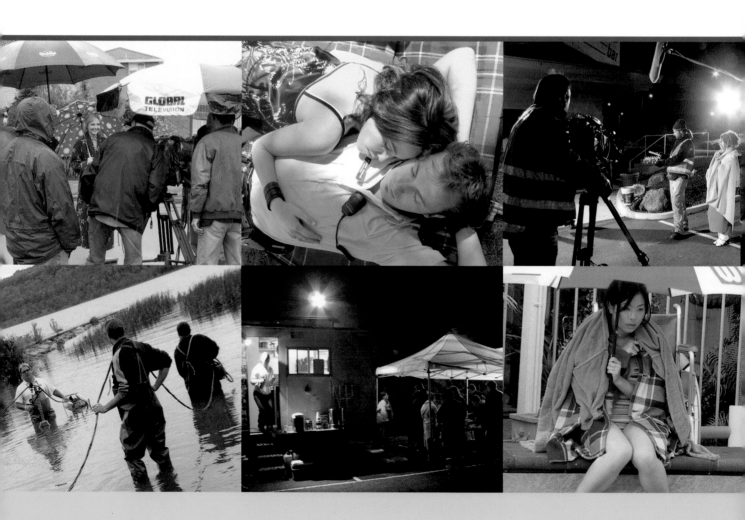

THIS PAGE: Blair McDonough and crew prepare to shoot Stuart's rodeo scenes on location. OPPOSITE CLOCKWISE FROM TOP: Marisa Warrington (Sindi Watts) waits beneath an umbrella between takes; Kym Valentine and Blair McDonough relax together off screen; the crew films on location at night; Michelle Ang waits miserably to shoot a sunny pool scene in the freezing cold; the catering van draws a crowd of cast and crew during a night shoot; the camera crew, wearing wetsuits, shoot a scene in the water.

LEFT: First assistant director Ryan Eckersley ponders a script. MIDDLE: The director, Nicholas Bufalo, follows along. RIGHT: Actors Madeleine West, Carla Bonner, Janet Andrewartha and Kym Valentine wait for the next take on set.

In the studio

Time and budget constraints mean that about two-thirds of *Neighbours* is filmed on set, at Global Television Studios, in Melbourne's east.

Monday and Wednesday are spent in rehearsals. On the other three weekdays, the actors are called to hair and makeup about an hour before they are due on "the floor".

A typical day of filming lasts 12 hours. If it is in the studio there are three cameras operating simultaneously; on location there is usually one. The session yields between 20 and 27 scenes, or 25 to 32 minutes of screen time.

"You do fly by the seat of your pants," says Stefan Dennis, who has played Paul Robinson for eight years in two stints, separated by a 12-year gap. "You do have to come up with the goods, and there is not a lot of time to come up with the goods."

What the television audience will hear Paul Robinson say, in four months, Stefan Dennis will have practised

about 10 times – three at home, another three or four during official rehearsal, and then a few more before the final shooting.

"And then, if there's a technical fault, or an actor fluffs the lines, we'll do it again," he says.

But as well as learning lines, the actors can tweak them in the name of character development.

"Nobody knows the character like I do, even the people who devised the character originally," Stefan says. "So if it's going to make the scene flow more naturally, or if it's going to make the character a bit more realistic, because the writer has overlooked an idiosyncracy of the character, you do get that licence to make changes. You can run changes by the director."

Continuity is particularly important during the second week of filming.

If Susan Kennedy has been filmed, on location, walking from her car in Ramsay Street to her front door, it's not until a week later, in the studio, that she will be seen stepping inside her house. The wardrobe crew ensures viewers won't notice the difference. They

How Very Harold

It's not difficult to fathom Ian Smith's massive international popularity. For almost 18 years on *Neighbours*, Smith has played the show's rock of reliability — the fuddy duddy with a heart of gold, Harold Bishop.

When tourist buses pull up at the *Neighbours* studio in Nunawading, or Smith appears at a Neighbours meet-and-greet session at the Elephant and Wheelbarrow pub in St Kilda, fans make a beeline for the man who's renowned for wobbling his chin in moments of exasperation.

Asked why he feels he's so popular with fans, Smith responds in typically

> "When I first came it was only for 10 weeks, to be a friend for Madge, but it was a friendship that turned into a marriage"

unpretentious fashion. "I've been on the show so long that maybe the fans feel it's a bit like meeting Father Christmas" he says. "I think they go nuts because they feel they've grown up with me.

"It really is fun to go to those backpackers' nights at the pub. There are 300-odd people there and people say all kinds of things to me.

"Some of them blame me for failing at university because they say they were watching *Neighbours* when they should have been studying. Sometimes fans get off the plane from England and don't even go to their hotel for a rest. They just jump straight on a bus and come to visit the place where *Neighbours* is made. Their passion for the show is unbelievable."

Smith, who joined the show in its second year, is justifiably proud of his place in its history.

"When I first came in it was only supposed to be for 10 weeks, to be a friend for Madge (Anne Charleston), but it was a friendship that turned into a marriage," he says.

In 1992, Smith was given his marching orders from the show. Madge — and Harold's legion of fans — were left to mourn the tragedy of him disappearing after being washed into treacherous surf. The soap later challenged the boundaries of believability when Ramsay Street matriarch Helen Daniels (Anne Haddy) saw Harold working in a Salvation Army op shop.

It turned out that after being swept out to sea, Harold had been picked up by a fishing trawler and taken to Tasmania where he was treated for amnesia to no avail before getting on with his life under a new name, Ted. Helen reunited him with Madge, his memory came back and he's been in Erinsborough ever since.

By mid-2004, Smith was worried about scriptwriters' plans for Harold. He wondered whether Harold's wayward behaviour after a stroke would stretch the character's credibility past breaking point. But his research on strokes and how they affect the psyche eased his worries. "There is nothing more important in acting than honesty and it was a challenge finding that honesty while all this mayhem was going on with Harold."

Smith has impressed with an ability to bring depth and texture to his role, but confesses there are days acting does not come easily to him. He can be plagued by an anxiety disorder, he says. "If I'm having a bad day with it I will go to the director and say, 'I think I'm going to need a bit of help today.' I have a wonderful GP and I once

said to him, 'Why am I stuck with this bloody anxiety?' He says it's because I'm an artist and acting's my outlet. Sometimes, everything overwhelms me and I can't handle it.

"I'm lucky to have good friends in the cast, who help me. We call it (anxiety) the black dog. When I read that actor Garry McDonald suffers from this, too, I suddenly thought, 'Thank God I'm not alone.' You can be in a crowded room, but if that black dog is after you, you feel so lonely.

"But I love coming to work here, even though my health is not what it used to be. When you turn 50, you realise your body can't do what it used to and when you turn 60 you're absolutely sure of it. I have bad knees and arthritis and I'm reminded of that every day."

He has long given up worrying whether being so widely known for playing Harold has denied him the opportunity to play other parts.

"The producers here will try to accommodate it if you ask for time to do a play or something and the desire to do that is still in me," he says. "But I cannot complain. Playing Harold, I do get challenged week after week as an actor."

A Week in the Life of Ian Smith

>>> Sunday >>> Begins with a half-hour session on the exercise bike, then get some breakfast for (wife) Gail. I have the *Neighbours* script for the week ahead. I'd have been given this script two weeks ago, but now it's time to reacquaint myself with it. It's important for me at this point to work out what scenes I'll be doing in the days ahead, make some notes on the script on what has happened in the lead-up to the scenes and at what time those events happened. If I know why I'm in the scene, it makes sense that it will be easier to do the scene. The rest of Sunday is relaxation time. Go to a nursery to look for some plants for the garden. I'm not a good cook, but I can do a roast and Gail and I sit down for dinner with a nice bottle of white wine.

>>> Monday >>> Up at 7am for a ride on the bike, make breakfast for Gail, then head to the studios in Nunawading for rehearsals starting at 8.45. There are always time pressures when you make as much TV a week as we do (2.5 hours).

When rehearsals are done in the afternoon I head to Dingley golf course to play nine holes. I meet this 83-year-old farmer on the course and he cleans me up! I am shocking.

It's not uncommon for some of the kids on the show to play a round of golf with me, time and work schedule permitting.

In the evening at home I work on my dialogue in the script. Gail hears me recite the words, but I don't act it out, so to speak. My thing is to get all the words into my head first, before I worry about the actual performance side of things. I feel that you've got to get the words into your head before you try to make those words work, otherwise it won't seem natural on the screen and people can see that you're acting.

Monday nights are when some of us cast go to meet fans at backpackers' nights at the Elephant and Wheelbarrow pub in St Kilda. About 300 people are there. It's a meet-and-greet situation with fans and it's a lot of fun.

>>> Tuesday >>> Normal routine, bike and get breakfast for Gail. I stick to this ritual because I'm a bit grumpy first thing in the morning and it's best for Gail if she doesn't come near me!

Tuesday is an OB (outside broadcast) and studio-shooting day, so it's a 6.30am start for me. The weather is hot and it's bloody hard work because we have to shoot around a hot barbecue. Talk about sweat. My skin is leaking. The make-up people have to keep sponging us down. It can also be hard in the winter, when working in the cold can be a real killer. Before shooting, I change into Harold's gear in the wardrobe bus. Nothing glamorous about having to do that. Unlike the others in the cast, I don't wear make-up because my skin reacts to it. If necessary, the make-up artist might just use a little powder to take the shine away.

Tuesday is the nitty gritty day. On this day I rush off a couple of times to go over words in the script. But you don't want to overdo this, otherwise filming it will be too mechanical.

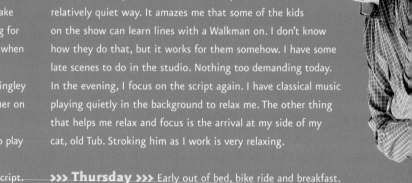

>>> Wednesday >>> Another rehearsal and shooting day, so climb out of bed at 7am for the bike ride, make Gail breakfast, then head into work. I like to learn my lines and work on scripts in a relatively quiet way. It amazes me that some of the kids on the show can learn lines with a Walkman on. I don't know how they do that, but it works for them somehow. I have some late scenes to do in the studio. Nothing too demanding today. In the evening, I focus on the script again. I have classical music playing quietly in the background to relax me. The other thing that helps me relax and focus is the arrival at my side of my cat, old Tub. Stroking him as I work is very relaxing.

>>> Thursday >>> Early out of bed, bike ride and breakfast. Shooting in studio and OB. My favourite work day of the week. I'm so chuffed to be working with the cast on this show. Even though we live in a world where kids think they know everything, it's nice that the young ones on the show will come to you for advice.

Evening is spent at home and looking at script. I do a bit of meditation because sometimes life can overwhelm me a bit and I suffer from anxiety attacks. I also sit and enjoy my new 51cm TV. I'm a documentary freak, and love English dramas.

>>> Friday >>> Up at 6am for bike ride and breakfast and feeling pretty good because all the production problems for the week have been ironed out. I have seven big scenes to film, which is a nice challenge. The most I've ever had was 23 scenes in one day — almost one entire episode.

Friday nights are a good release. There's some real musical talent on this show and I go to a gig to see Natalie Bassingthwaighte (who plays Izzy Hoyland) perform with her band. Boy, can Natalie sing.

>>> Saturday >>> Very relaxing day. No rush to get out of bed early. I love orchids. They are my hobby, so I love spending time in the garden. In the afternoon, I pour myself a single-malt, get outside, and trim the dead leaves away and feed the orchids. I enjoy a trip into the country with Gail. I like to go to Kyneton and get the fly-fishing rod out and try to catch a brown trout. Sometimes I'll also take a little cray pot with me and try to bring home a yabby. ●

Putting it all together

would make extensive notes and take photos of Jackie Woodburne to make sure Susan's earrings are the same, that the same number of cardigan buttons are done up, and that her handbag is on the same shoulder.

But continuity is also the responsibility of the actors, and Carla Bonner (Steph Scully) says this is where knowing the script back-to-front is crucial. "You don't want to be on location crying and then walk onto set (a week later) for the next scene and forget your character was crying a few seconds ago," Carla says.

Once filming has finished, a block of *Neighbours* is far from complete, and is still several months away from our lounge rooms.

First, the editors put the studio and location shots in order. Ultimately, each episode of *Neighbours* must last between 22 minutes, 30 seconds and 22 minutes 45 seconds, which sometimes means trimming several minutes from the original cut.

"When you are throwing away four minutes, it's

ABOVE LEFT: Ryan Moloney shoots a court scene on location as Toadfish Rebecchi.
ABOVE RIGHT : Tom Oliver waits as the first assistant director, Ryan Eckersley claps the first take of a new scene.
BELOW: A bird's eye view of the *Neighbours* studio, where the second week of shooting takes place.

FROM FAR LEFT: Cast and crew prepare a scene on location. Post-production supervisor Sue Washington. The OB crew films a scene on location.

When Steph Scully unzips her leather jacket, what the audience hears is a sauce bottle being squashed

quite devastating," says post-production supervisor Sue Washington. "It's a lot of work that people have done that never gets seen. And it's a lot of money."

Conversely, if an episode winds up being short, writers are sent back to the scripting board and actors to the set, and a new scene is slotted into the storyline.

The preparation is so streamlined that the first version of each episode usually comes in closer to the ideal: between 45 seconds and two minutes over time.

This buffer gives the producer and directors footage to tinker with. Over five days, scenes can be rearranged, excess lines removed, and characters' pauses erased.

Lighting is also adjusted so that scenes shot hours apart on location follow seamlessly on screen. Dull days can even be made to look brighter (in keeping with the policy that Erinsborough enjoys summer endlessly).

After the opening and closing credits are added, the result is an episode of *Neighbours* fit for television ... in silence.

Sound still needs to be added to the vision, and that's done on three levels. To enable non-English-speaking countries to apply their own dubbing – Neighbours is simulcast to almost 60 countries – the English dialogue must be removable.

"Once we pull the dialogue away, all the other effects are still there," Sue explains. "They are left with all the stepping sounds and body rustles and chinking glasses."

Did you know?

Neighbours is not shown during the Christmas period in Australia so episodes involving Christmas celebrations are rarely featured. Less than 10 Christmases have been celebrated on screen in the show's 20-year history.

These incidental noises are artificial, and form another layer of audio.

When Drew Kirk (Dan Paris) and Stuart Parker (Blair McDonough) took to the rodeo, their stunt doubles were filmed in silence.

"We replaced nearly all of the sounds – all of the saddle noises, the jiggles of the bridles, all of the hoofs, the snorting and neighing of the horses, the gate opening, the cattle sounds, the crowd cheering, the music for the carousel, the PA announcer and the whip cracking," Sue says.

Like every other non-speaking noise on *Neighbours*, they were individually recorded and added to the vision. One by one, they brought the mute footage to life.

Some sounds are recorded from the source, such as the scanner in the general store. But others are manufactured. When Steph Scully (Carla Bonner) unzips her leather jacket, for example, what the audience hears is the recording of a sauce bottle being squashed.

"We can get a bit of the natural sound on tape, but to make it dramatic, you've got to enhance all those things," Sue says.

Music – and there are up to 80 pieces in five episodes – is the last layer of audio added to the block's master tape.

Extensive technical testing is done, and captioning for the deaf is added, before the 112-minute package is finally sold to the world.

And each time the show's 120 million viewers catch up on the Ramsay Street residents' exploits, there will be seven people in a Melbourne office plotting the next eight months of installations. ●

The Neighbours Game

"The Hilarious Game based on the Exciting Characters from Ramsay Street"

FOR TWO TO EIGHT PLAYERS. AGES NINE TO ADULT

Neighbours — *The First 10 Years*

LASSITERS

A CARD GAME THE WHOLE NEIGHBOURHOOD CAN PLAY

Neighbours CARD GAME

An A–Z of Neighbours

Everything you'll ever need to know about Ramsay Street, from Amnesia to Xmas decoration wars. By Tony Johnston

Official *Neighbours* memorabilia including the Christmas album and the *Neighbours* board game.

A

AFL footy

AMNESIA The soapie scriptwriter's favorite device. Mrs Mangel (Vivean Grey) got it when she fell down a ladder while painting Daphne's nursery; Susan (Jackie Woodburne) suffered an extreme case of it after slipping on some spilt milk and banging her head; Harold (Ian Smith) had it for five years after disappearing at the seashore.

ARMY Ryan McLachlan (Richard Norton) joined the army; so did Stuart (Chooka – Blair McDonough).

ABORTION Phoebe (Simone Robertson) considered having one; so did Lori (Michelle Ang) before fleeing to New Zealand.

AFL FOOTY Paul McClain (Jansen Spencer) was invited to try out with one of the Melbourne clubs, before finally moving to Adelaide to join the Crows.

B

BIGAMY Michael Daniels' (Brian Blain) marriage to Helen Daniels (Anne Haddy) was annulled when it was discovered he was already married.

BACKPACKERS Toadfish (Ryan Moloney) and Lance (Andrew Bibby) wanted to set up a backpackers' hostel at No.30.

BANK ROBBERY Julie Robinson (Vikki Blanche) was caught up in one when the Pacific Bank was robbed; so were Stuart, Sindi and Toadfish.

BRAIN TUMOR Lucy (Melissa Bell) was diagnosed with one; so was Boyd Hoyland (Kyal Marsh).

BOMBS Dr. Karl's surgery was bombed, and there was a bomb scare at Erinsborough High.

BLACKMAIL Todd Landers' (Kristian Schmid) father Bob tried to blackmail Helen Daniels; Susan was blackmailed by Gareth Rivers; Tahnee Coppin (Anna Jennings Edquist) tried to blackmail Connor (Patrick Harvey) then Nina (Delta Goodrem); Izzy offered to pay Darcy not to tell the Kennedys that her baby wasn't Karl's.

BUSHFIRE Cody Willis (Peta Brady) went missing during a bushfire and a body was found, but then so was she; Joe Scully's (Shane Connor) taxi was caught in middle of a bushfire and he helped deliver his passenger's baby.

BORN TO TRY Nina's hit song crosses over to become a No.1 for Delta Goodrem on the Australian record charts.

BOB THE DOG Toadfish sent a Bob "substitute" to his owner Sarah in England.

BOLLYWOOD Nina returned from India's film centre a star.

BOAT Izzy (Natalie Bassingthwaighte) fell out of one and nearly drowned when Karl proposed.

Backpackers tour Ramsay St

Delta Goodrem, author of *Born To Try*.

Daphne in a coma.

Darwin at sunset.

C

COUNCIL (ERINSBOROUGH) Those who made it on to the council were Madge (Anne Charleston) and Lou (Tom Oliver), who was briefly Mayor; and David Bishop (Kevin Harrington). Evan Hancock (Nicholas Opolski) ran against Joe Scully and won, with support from Joe's own daughter, Michelle (Kate Keltie). When Julie Martin (Julie Mullins) ran for council she won three votes.

CANCER Those who suffered or died from cancer in the show have included Madge, Ruth (Ailsa Piper), school principal Dorothy Burke (Maggie Dence); Steph (Carla Bonner), and Annalise (Kimberly Davies), who had skin cancer but recovered after surgery.

CARAVAN Charlene (Kylie Minogue) lived in one behind Lassiters for a time; so did Sarah Beaumont (Nicola Charles); Lou hid Lolly (Jiordan Anna Tolli) in a caravan park; and Stuart found Jamie Clarke (Angus McLaren) in a caravan park.

COMA Daphne (Elaine Smith) was in a coma for a time after a car crash coming back from her father's funeral, and before she died; Toadfish was discovered in a coma in hospital after he had been missing for some time; Darcy (Mark Rafferty) slipped into one after falling down stairs; Boyd Hoyland (Kyal Marsh) was in a coma for a while as a result of a brain tumour.

CITIZEN OF THE YEAR Harold won this Erinsborough title.

CEREBRAL ANEURYSM After Madge recovered from a cerebral aneurysm in hospital, she and Harold were ready to leave. Harold asked, "Don't we need clearance or something?", to which Madge replied, "Harold, I'm not an aircraft".

CHEATING Toadfish accused Taj Coppin (Jamie Robbie Reyne) of cheating at his school exams.

D

DUCKS Surely one of the most imaginative deaths for a soapie star ever: Harold's daughter and Joe's wife, Kerry (Linda Hartley) was accidentally shot dead while protesting against duck-shooting season.

DJs Tad Reeves (Jonathon Dutton) played his first DJ gig at the club Hemisfear. Henry Ramsay (Craig McLachlan) became a radio DJ in New Zealand.

DINING TABLE Dr Clive Gibbons (Geoff Paine) performed an emergency operation on Lucy (Kylie Flinker) on the Robinson's dining table.

DRUGS Brad Willis (Scott Michaelson) was arrested for drug smuggling. Cody Willis was killed in a drug siege.

DRINK DRIVING Helen Daniels was charged with DD; Doctor Karl (Alan Fletcher) was breathalised, blew over the limit and lost his licence.

DARWIN Doug and Pam Willis (Terence Donovan and Sue Jones) moved there; Rick Alessi (Dan Falzon) took a job there; the Martins moved there.

DANGEROUS DRIVING Matt Hancock (Stephen Hunt) was charged after the crash that injured himself, Leo (Anthony Hammer) and Harold.

DVD PLAYERS Lou ended up selling dodgy ones to Rosie's (Maggie Millar) parishioners on a day outing.

DAYTIME SOAPS Oscar Scully (Ingo Dammer-Smith) was addicted to them for a time; Libby Kennedy (Kym Valentine) won a date with the star of her favourite soap and ended up spending a passionate night in his hotel.

E

ERINSBOROUGH The fictional suburb in which the *Neighbours* characters live. Originally named Erinsfield.

EXPELLED Danni Stark (Eliza Szonert) was expelled from Erinsborough High; Lucy Robinson was expelled from boarding school.

G

GORILLA Daphne's kidnapper wore a gorilla suit.

GRUNDY (REG) The founder of Grundy who commissioned Reg Watson to create *Neighbours*, and who subsequently sold it to the world.

GOSSIP Every show needs its resident gossip. First there was Mrs Mangel and then Madge; now the new age version is Summer Hoyland (Marisa Siketa).

GRAFFITI Nick Page (Mark Stevens) was caught spraying graffiti on Jim Robinson's workshop; Denny Cook (Katie Ditchburn) did Lou's garage and the 40-Hour Foxtrot; Zack did some to show his love for Michelle Scully; Saxon Garvey (Troy Lovett) spray-painted the walls at No.30.

GAMBLING Toby Mangel (Ben Geurens) was encouraged to gamble by Michael (Troy Beckwith); Rosie was forced to go to Gambler's Anonymous; Darcy lost a large amount at the Aurora Club; Lance Wilkinson also had a problem with it.

GO-GO DANCER Lucy worked as one in a club.

GARAGE Where Charlene worked as a mechanic; Valda (Joan Sydney) ended up living in the Scullys' garage.

GRAPPA GIRL The demeaning job offered to Flick (Holly Valance) trawling nightclubs in a skimpy outfit.

GAY Harold had to kiss Valda to prove he wasn't gay.

GET SMART Karl and Izzy share a passion for the old American spy sitcom.

F

FAMILIES Famous neighbourhood families have been Ramsay, Robinson, Bishop, Mangel, Scully, Carpenter, Clarke, Daniels, Willis, Alessi, Gottlieb, Hancock, Hartman, Hoyland, Kennedy, Martin, Rebecchi, Stark and Wilkinson.

FISHY NAMES Four characters have had fishy nicknames – Stonefish (Anthony Engleman), Toadfish, Tadpole and Stingray (Ben Nicholas).

FREEZER Josh (Jeremy Angerson) and Melissa (Jade Amenta) were locked in Lassiters' freezer overnight.

FIRE Lou and Rosie were kissing in the church while it was on fire.

FULL MONTY Amy trained the males of Ramsay Street for their charity version of *The Full Monty*.

The Full Monty comes to Ramsay Street.

Reg Grundy

House fire during the millennium party.

H

HOME JAMES The chauffeur-driven car business owned by Helen Daniels.

HEART ATTACK Mrs Mangel, Karl Kennedy and Harold survived one; Jim Robinson (Alan Dale) didn't.

HOUSE FIRE The Ramsay house went up in smoke with Harold inside; Brad saved Beth and Hannah Martin (Rebecca Ritters) from a house fire; Madge was caught in a fire at No.24; Lolly was rescued when the Scully house burnt down during the millennium street party.

HAROLD'S FOOD FLINGING FRENZY A game on the BBC *Neighbours* website, where the aim is to serve customers their orders quickly. If you fail, The Coffee Shop blows up. See the game at: http://www.bbc.co.uk/neighbours/games/.

PASSPORT

Connor could have used one of these.

I

IMMIGRATION Michelle and her Irish boy Connor were on the run from the immigration authorities at one stage.

INFERTILE Steph Scully discovered the reason she couldn't have kids was that Max Hoyland (Stephen Lovatt) was infertile.

IVF Max and Steph gave it a go in their quest for a baby.

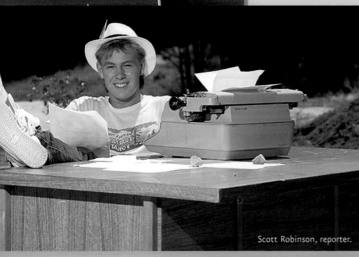

Scott Robinson, reporter.

Filming Harold's coronation as King of Erinsborough Fair.

K

J

JOURNALISTS Three characters were or are journalists – Scott Robinson, Libby Kennedy and Sindi Watts.

JOB REFERENCE Sarah Beaumont phoned former boss and lover Dr Karl from London for a reference just as he was remarrying Susan.

KIDNAPPED Six separate characters have been kidnapped or taken hostage – Helen Daniels, Lucy Robinson, Toadfish, Cheryl Stark (Caroline Gillmer), Bouncer the dog, and Daphne by a man in a gorilla suit.

KARMA The name of Hannah's horse, a birthday surprise.

KING OF ERINSBOROUGH FAIR A title won by Harold.

LASSITERS HOTEL The hotel and retail complex at the heart of the Erinsborough community.

LABOUR IN UNUSUAL PLACES Daphne, at a picnic; Libby, in a barn at a rodeo; and Christina Alessi Robinson (Gayle Blakeney), in an icecream van.

LESBIANS The show controversially introduced a lesbian relationship between Sky Mangel (Stephanie McIntosh) and guest character Lana Crawford (Bridget Neval).

LOGIES These are Australia's major television awards and *Neighbours* has won 22 Logie Awards, including the Gold Logie for Most Popular Personality (Kylie Minogue, Craig McLachlan), Most Popular Actress (Annie Jones, Rachel Friend and Kylie Minogue twice in a row); Most Popular Actor (Jason Donovan, Craig McLachlan twice in a row and Peter O'Brien twice in a row); Most Popular Drama, Most Popular Series, Most Popular New Talent (Peter O'Brien, Brooke Satchwell, Patrick Harvey, Daniel MacPherson, Delta Goodrem and Natalie Blair); Reg Grundy (founder of Grundy Television) was inducted into the Hall of Fame and in 2005, so was *Neighbours* itself.

LOTTO Madge and Harold won big on lotto and toured abroad. Later, Angie Rebecchi also won.

LIFE MECHANICS Jonathan Verne's (Oscar Redding's) bogus self-improvement course.

LIFESTYLE TV The Scullys are chosen to participate in a lifestyle renovation show.

LINGERIE PARTY Sindi and Sky threw one and spiced up the romance on Ramsay Street.

LONG QT SYNDROME A hereditary heart condition thought to have killed Max Hoyland's first wife, Anna-Claire, and also afflicts their daughter Summer.

MEMORABILIA There are some exciting variations of *Neighbours* memorabilia (see page 174) including a board game, several DVDs, albums, novellas, and commemorative stamps produced by Australia Post.

MODELLING Four characters tried professional modeling at some stage – Sarah Beaumont, Jane Harris (Annie Jones), Sam Kratz (Richard Grieve) and Lucy Robinson, while Toadfish, Stuart and Connor got a one-off modelling gig.

MILLENNIUM PARTY Surely the Ramsay Street party to end all parties – the Scullys' house burnt down, Amy (Jacinta Stapleton) was exposed for cheating on Lance and Drew (Dan Paris) proposed to Libby.

MUSEUM Melbourne Museum contains the original set of the kitchen that played home to the Robinson, Martin and Scully families.

MOTORBIKES Gemma Ramsay (Beth Buchanan) and Matt Robinson (Ashley Paske) were involved in a motorbike accident and Gemma nearly lost use of a leg; Libby Kennedy and Steph Scully had a motorbike accident; Mike Young also owned one.

MENINGITIS Daphne once contracted it, and Sharon Davies (Jessica Muschamp) broke up with Nick Page when he came down with it.

MISSING Harold went missing, presumed dead; Emily Hancock (Isabella Oldham) also briefly went missing; as did Steph; Susan went missing after losing her memory, and Karl was thought responsible; Toadfish also went missing for a while.

MISCARRIAGE Dee Bliss (Madeleine West) had one; Izzy faked a miscarriage to fire Karl up; later the baby was stillborn when Izzy fell down the stairs.

MEN OF ERINSBOROUGH CALENDAR Rosie's fundraising idea.

MANURE Sarah Beaumont sent a truckload to the Kennedy House when she heard Karl and Susan had remarried.

MAKING MANSIONS The name of the reality renovation show that starred the Scullys.

A panorama of the Lassiters complex prior to the 2004 fire.

N

NEW ZEALAND Where Henry (Craig McLachlan) and Bronwyn (Rachel Friend) moved to; Bess Robinson (June Salter) also went there.

NUDE PHOTOS Hannah found nude photos of Lucy in a magazine.

NUDE SCULPTURE Gino (Shane McNamara) bought one for Harold's house.

NARCOTICS ANONYMOUS Lou attended after becoming addicted to pain killers.

NEW VOICE The name of Libby's magazine.

NEW GUINEA Rosie went there after leaving Ramsay Street.

NEEDLE PHOBIA Max Hoyland's phobia was exposed when he began his role in Steph's IVF treatment.

New Zealand

O

ORANGES They spilled onto the floor and surrounded Jim when he was left for dead after his heart attack.

OVERDOSE Jill Weir (Lyn Semler) took one after her affair with Doug Wills ended.

ONLINE GIRLFRIENDS Toadfish and Connor pretended to be "online girlfriends" to strangers to make extra cash, and Connor's creation "Carol" became Lou's girlfriend.

Oranges

Darcy Tyler in prison.

PUNCH-UPS Memorable occasions included Charlene punching Scott (Jason Donovan) when they first met; Shane (Peter O'Brien) and Mike (Guy Pearce) having a boxing match over Jane Harris; Doug Willis punched Simon, who threatened to sue; Mal Kennedy (Benjamin McNair) punched Darren Stark (Scott Major) over Catherine O'Brien (Radha Mitchell); Drew Kirk was punched by Sandy Hutchens' husband; Drew punched Mike Healy (Andrew Blackman); unhappy with her marks, Jess Fielding (Elisa Gazdowicz) hit her teacher Susan Kennedy at school; Stuart Parker punched Marc Lambert and was arrested for it; Tahnee and Nina came to blows during their feud; Joe Scully (Shane Connor) taught Summer how to box.

PERTH Where Mike Young ended up. Brad and Beth (Natalie Imbruglia) settled there.

PILL Charlene caused a furore in 1987 when she asked Dr Clive Gibbons to put her on the Pill.

PSYCHIATRIC HOSPITAL Jill Weir was admitted to one after threatening to kill herself over her affair with Doug Willis; Gus Cleary (Ben Barrack) was also committed.

PRIVATE INVESTIGATOR Paul Robinson (Stefan Dennis) hired one to probe Lucy's manager/husband David Kazalian.

PRISON Darren Stark (Todd McDonald) did time; Tommy Roles (Tiber Gyapjas), who taught Harold the tuba, was a prison chaplain; Henry Ramsay (Craig McLachlan) did a stint in prison before arriving on Ramsay Street. Steph visited Larry Woodhouse (Andrew Curry) in prison; Matt Hancock was kept in remand after bail was refused on a dangerous driving charge; Darcy Tyler was held in remand for burglary of the Kennedy house; Lou was sentenced to two years' jail for fraud but got out after winning his appeal; Rocco Camenitti did time after kidnapping Toadie.

POISONED Connor accidentally poisoned Michelle Scully with floor cleaner.

PEEPING TOM Harold caught Boyd and Daniel (Thomas Blackburne) spying on the Scullys' bathroom.

PRANK PHONE CALLS They unsettled Karl and Dee (the culprits were later found to be Summer and Boyd).

PERIWINKLE EXTRACT Lou sold a counterfeit version in one of his scams.

POST-NATAL DEPRESSION Lyn Scully (Janet Andrewartha) suffered from it, which caused her to shoplift, among other things.

PERFORMANCE ANXIETY Harold suffered from it as his romance with Svetlanka (Deidre Rubenstein) intensified.

POST OFFICE The 2004 season ended with a huge cliff-hanger – the burning of the Lassiters complex, including the Coffee Shop. This provided the *Neighbours* production team with a fresh canvas to redevelop the set. Among the new buildings is a Post Office, which forms part of Lou and Harold's General Store. Production worked closely with Australia Post to create the store, which is an official, registered Post Office.

Q

QUOTES Probably the classic quote from the show, in relation to what ensued, was Annalise's (Kimberley Davies): "Can anyone else smell gas?" before the fire.

QUEENSLAND Where Charlene and Scott now live with their son Daniel; Madge joined them there for a few years after Harold disappeared; Billy and Anne (Jesse Spencer and Brooke Satchwell) also went to live together in Queensland.

R

RADIO Several residents were radio announcers, notably Henry Ramsay, Toadfish and Lou and Marlene.

ROBINSON FAMILY The key family throughout the history of *Neighbours*.

RAMSAY STREET Where all the key characters live.

RIO DE JANEIRO Where Paul Robinson fled to escape fraud charges (before his recent return).

RUN OVER Bouncer was run over a number of times and Cheryl Stark was hit when Julie Martin accidentally backed her car into Cheryl during an argument.

RED BALLOONS A heap of them were left outside No.30 for Sarah Beaumont.

RECIPES Madge put out a Ramsay Street recipe book, which Max rescued from the 2004 fire for Harold.

RAMSBOTTOM STREET The new name proposed for Ramsay Street – Harold led the fight to prevent it.

ROBBERY Ruby Dwyer's (Maureen Edwards) gambling problems forced her to have Harold's house robbed; Darcy Tyler robbed the pub to pay James; Darcy also robbed Susan and Karl's house.

ROBOT ANNIHILATION CHALLENGE Sindi and Connor competed in one.

Brisbane

The most famous street sign in Australia.

SCULLY FAMILY Their arrival in Ramsay Street brought a breath of fresh air to the series.

STRIPPER Daphne's job when first introduced to the boys of Ramsay Street at a buck's party.

SUPERMARKET What Paul Robinson planned to build once he bulldozed Ramsay Street.

SALVATION ARMY Harold was found playing the tuba in the Salvation Army band by Helen Daniels.

SNOWDROPPER Angie Rebecchi (Leslie Baker) stole Cheryl Stark's underwear off the washing line because she admired her clothes.

SHOOTING Terri Inglis-Robinson (Maxine Kiblingaitis) shot husband Paul Robinson; Kerry (Linda Hartman) was accidentally shot dead while protesting against duck shooting; Brad Willis was shot by Bob Landers who was holding Phoebe hostage; Malcolm Kennedy (Ben McNair) accidentally wounded Lou Carpenter; Cody Willis was shot and killed.

STEROIDS Guy Carpenter (Andrew Williams) was suspected of using them; and Paul McLain was offered them by Nathan Tyson on the footy team.

STOLEN CAR Phil Martin (Ian Rawlings) bought a car from Lou that turned out to be stolen.

STREET DRAG RACE Matt Robinson won money taking part in an illegal race.

STALKER Sarah Beaumont was stalked by Richard Downing; and Carmella Cammeniti (Natalie Blair) was stalked by a bodyguard.

SKATEBOARDERS Scott Robinson, Luke Dawson (Adrian Foley), Boyd Hoyland and Stingray.

SNAKES Stuart kept one named Harold as a pet. Phoebe Gottlieb (Simone Robertson) also owned one.

SWEDEN Elly Conway (Kendall Nunn) went to Sweden with mum Liz (Christine Keogh).

SEXUAL HARASSMENT Dee Bliss (Madeleine West) was the centre of the case involving Dr Cook.

SHARKS Lassiters barman Alex (Marco Pio Venturini) took Steph Scully swimming with sharks while on a date; later Darcy and Toadfish visited the same shark tank to hilarious effect; Brad Willis was attacked by a shark.

SPEED DATING Harold, Lou and Max Hoyland signed up for the event at the pub.

SAMURAI WARRIORS Valda turned the pub waiters into samurai warriors as part of a make-over.

SPELLS Summer cast one on Declan to have him break up with her.

STILL Josh Anderson blew up the science room at Erinsborough High while trying to make an alcohol still.

SNAILS Toby Mangel was paid by Doug Willis to collect them.

The Scully family.

T

TUBA Harold's preferred musical instrument.

TASMANIA Where Harold spent his lost years.

TEACHERS Characters who worked as teachers include Susan, Mike Young, Dorothy Burke, Libby Kennedy and Tess Bell. Paul Robinson got a teaching degree while in prison.

TRUTH OR DARE The game they were playing when Toadfish first kissed future wife Dee Bliss.

TATTOO Stingray has one with the name "Shazza" (which he claims was his pet hamster as a kid).

TRANSPLANT Harold offered the ailing Lou one of his kidneys; Liljana Bishop (Marcella Russo) discovered she needed a new liver to survive, and was only saved when her lost son Luka (Keelan O'Hehir) donated a portion of his liver.

TANGO Lyn Scully and son-in-law Max took lessons.

Salamanca market in Hobart.

U

UK Those characters who moved to the UK after leaving Erinsborough included Mrs Nell Mangel, Jane Harris, Sarah Beaumont, Annalise Hartman, Sam Kratz, Nick Page, Joe Mangel and wife Melanie (Lucinda Cowden).

UNFAIR DISMISSAL Libby sued *The Chronicle* when they sacked her for being pregnant.

ULTRASOUND Izzy tried to fake one to prove to Karl she was having his baby.

V

VIDEO TAPE Helen Daniels played a video tape of Charlene and Scott's wedding to help end the feud between the Bishops and the Martins; Dr Karl set up a video camera to catch whoever was putting rubbish in his wheelie bin; Stephen Gottlieb (Lochie Daddo) fainted while watching Phoebe's birth video.

VASECTOMY Benito Alessi (George Spartels) secretly had one.

VICAR Rosie the vicar was pursued by both Lou and Harold.

The Alessi Family

135

W

WEDDINGS There have been some great weddings over 20 years - The first ever wedding on *Neighbours* was when Paul Robinson married Terri Inglis after one date; Daphne and Des married in a traditional church ceremony; Charlene sang at her grandparents' wedding; Paul and Gail initially married for business reasons; Gloria married Gail's father, Rob Lewis, who ran the car yard; Charlene and Scott's wedding was a momentous day; also Jim and Beverly; Harold and Madge; Mrs Mangel and John Worthington; Joe Mangel and Kerry Bishop; Paul married again, this time to Christina; Helen married Michael; Joe married Melanie; Stephen married Phoebe; Brad married Beth; Mark nearly married Annalise; Helen married Reuben White; Rob married Jo; Philip married Ruth; Sarah married Peter; Drew married Libby; Marc married Stephanie; Karl and Susan renewed their vows; Toadie and Dee married; Lou married Trixie; Max married Steph; and Valda Sheargold married Charlie Cassidy after Steph and Max's wedding.

WAKE When Paul Robinson left the wake of his wife Gail's father, it was the beginning of the end for their marriage.

THE WIGGLES Visited Ramsay Street after Drew took Lolly Carpenter to see them.

X

XMAS DECORATION WARS Erupt regularly in Ramsay Street, as one house tries to outdo the other.

Y

YACHT Charlie Cassidy owned a yacht.

Z

ZOO Joe Mangel and Kerry Bishop married in the Butterfly Enclosure at Melbourne Zoo.

The Wiggles

Lou always gets into the Xmas spirit.

Neighbours — CARL RUHEN — HORWITZ GRAHAME

Neighbours — CARL RUHEN — HORWITZ GRAHAME

Neighbours — CARL RUHEN — HORWITZ GRAHAME

A CARD GAME

Neighbours™ CARD·GAME

The First 10 Years — JOSEPHINE MONROE

Neighbours

"The Hilarious Game based on the Exciting Characte

Neighbours™ Game

Brighter Lights

Neighbours has been
the first step on the road
to world stardom for
many actors.

By Tony Johnston

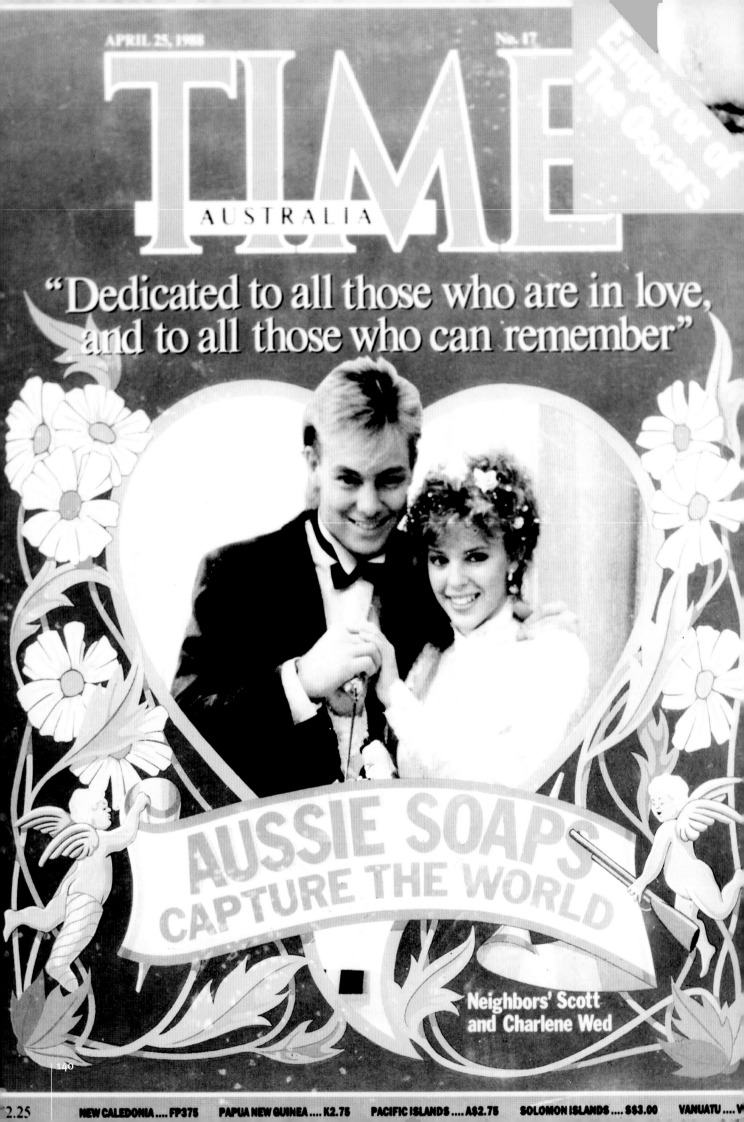

APRIL 25, 1988   No. 17

TIME

AUSTRALIA

"Dedicated to all those who are in love, and to all those who can remember"

AUSSIE SOAPS CAPTURE THE WORLD

Neighbors' Scott and Charlene Wed

2.25   NEW CALEDONIA .... FP375   PAPUA NEW GUINEA .... K2.75   PACIFIC ISLANDS .... A$2.75   SOLOMON ISLANDS .... S$3.00   VANUATU V

The number of *Neighbours* alumni who have made it big on the world stage is quite staggering, given the modest pretensions of the TV drama – it is, after all, a five nights-a-week soap!

"When the show started we just wanted success in Australia," says the long-time casting director of *Neighbours*, Jan Russ, also celebrating 20 years on the job.

Neighbours creator Reg Watson has said that his model was the long-running British soap *Coronation Street*, but says he infused very Australian differences: a younger, fresh-faced cast; Aussie open-natured sensibilities; and good communication between adults and teenagers.

This magic ingredient – giving teenagers prominent roles in everyday adult life – was the hook for young viewers everywhere. And it created an acting template for an endless stream of aspiring young Australian actors.

More importantly, it was never considered uncool for an actor to have done a stint on *Neighbours*.

Veteran actor Terence Donovan, who played Doug Willis, attributes the show's longevity to its ability from the earliest days to capture young audiences, through such characters as those played by Kylie Minogue, his son Jason and Craig McLachlan.

Neighbours debuted in the UK in October 1986, but it was not until the beginning of 1988 that "*Neighbours* fever" hit there. There was no stopping the rollercoaster.

In the years to follow, many of the rising young stars made the (Australian) summer trek to the UK to star in pantomimes, earning big bucks and making more people aware of their Australian soap.

Guy Pearce got his start in *Neighbours* and is now a Hollywood heavyweight. "I often talk about the *Neighbours* time in England like Beatlemania," he said to *Film 2000*. "England was looking for something at that time, that was relaxed and chilled out and had lots of sunshine, and this, that and the other; and *Neighbours* came along and that was it. Suddenly it

PREVIOUS PAGE: Kylie Minogue launches an exhibition of her costumes at the Melbourne Arts Centre earlier this year.

OPPOSITE: The cover of Australia's April 5, 1988 *Time* magazine features Scott and Charlene's wedding. **FAR LEFT:** Terence and Jason Donovan, the father and son team who starred on *Neighbours*. **LEFT:** Stephanie McIntosh, who plays Sky Mangel, is Jason Donovan's half-sister.

took off and there were 20 million people watching it – it was just crazy, you know!"

Jan Russ, who helped compile the following list, goes to pains to point out that it was not just the popularity of the show that drove the careers of those who made it big.

"Look at the list, and I can tell you the one thing that stands out for me is that they were all focused – there's not a prima donna among them," she says. "It wasn't just the producers, the directors, the writers … these young people were all disciplined and professional, and that goes a long way."

Russ is still in contact with many of the actors she gave a start to, and of course, she delights in their success.

Having cast nearly all of them, she finds it hard to single out people, but she mentions the obvious: Jason, Guy, Daniel (MacPherson), Nat (Imbruglia), Jesse (Spencer).

"The other was Russell (Crowe), although he was only a guest on the show. But there was something about him. The problem was he had other commitments and so could only spare a couple of weeks."

One that did get away was Hugh Jackman. "I'd signed him and just when he was about to start, he came and told me he'd been accepted into WAAPA (the prestigious Western Australian Academy of

The woman mechanic, fact or fiction?

Performing Arts), so we let him go.

"After he graduated he came and auditioned again as part of doing the rounds, but I think he'd already committed to *Correlli* (the ABC drama series that launched his career). He was another one who had it all; he was a real charmer."

Russ won't name favourites, but you can't help but get the impression she has a soft spot for MacPherson and Minogue.

"When I went to England for a trip last year I visited (MacPherson) on the set of *The Bill*. He took me around and introduced me to everyone – and he knew everyone. There's no huge ego involved with that boy; he's pleasant and charming. And he has the talent."

Of Kylie, she says: "What she's done with her career is just extraordinary. Not just her acting; she became a style icon for her age group. She created a glamour for the young ones when they were going through that scruffy era of late '80s.

"She's pure showbiz. As Betty Pounder (legendary dance teacher) used to say: 'Sparkle, darling' ... and she (Kylie) always did. Plus she keeps reinventing herself. In a way, she's another Cher," says Russ.

And she means it as a huge compliment.

Here, then, is a list of some former *Neighbours* stars who have made the Big Time:

Guy Pearce

NEIGHBOURS CHARACTER: MIKE YOUNG

Initially a student and worker in the coffee shop before becoming a teacher, Mike was also a photographer. A school friend of Scott Robinson (Jason Donovan) he moved in with Des (Paul Keane) and Daphne (Elaine Smith). He had the hots for Jane (Annie Jones) but eventually she turned to Des, so Mike took off to Perth to look after his sick mum.

CAREER SINCE

Guy has become possibly the most sought-after actor from the series. After leaving *Neighbours* he did a short stint in rival soap *Home And Away* and made a handful of Aussie movies, among them *Hunting* and *Friday On My Mind*, before catching everyone's eye with his brave and outrageous performance as a drag queen in *The Adventures of Priscilla, Queen Of The Desert*. It gave him an entrée to Hollywood, and yet his next role couldn't have been more different – playing a bespectacled cop caught up in a web of corruption with Russell Crowe and Kevin Spacey in *LA Confidential*.

The film was a huge critical success, drawing comparisons with *Chinatown*, although it was only moderately successful at the box office. It opened countless doors for Pearce, but his choices of projects since have verged on eccentric — from challenging pieces such as *Memento* to popcorn movies such as *The Count Of Monte Cristo* and *The Time Machine*. His latest projects include the films *First Snow*, *I Believe In America* and *Dangerous Parking*. He has also done short seasons of theatre, most notably in a Melbourne Theatre Company production of *Sweet Bird of Youth*.

QUOTABLE

"It was such an incredible launching pad. I was there for four years and I was quite meticulous at observing what I was doing and what everyone else was doing … so it was a really good training ground." – *Film 2000*

TOP: Peter O'Brien in TV series *White Collar Blue*.
MIDDLE: Guy Pearce in *Two Brothers*.
OPPOSITE: Alan Dale in US series *24*.

Neighbours Nicknames

Some of the best nicknames:

1 *Charlene's nickname for journalist boyfriend Scott was 'Scoop'.*

2 *Toadfish, Stonefish, and Stingray are all nicknames.*

3 *Stuart Parker is called Chooka.*

4 *Lou's nickname for Harold – Jelly Belly – triggered a return of Harold's memory.*

5 *Sarah Beaumont's childhood nickname was Froggy.*

Peter O'Brien

NEIGHBOURS CHARACTER: SHANE RAMSAY

One of the original cast, Shane was a member of the founding Ramsay Family. He worked in the Erinsborough bank with Des Clarke (Paul Keane), who he lost out to in winning the hand of Daphne (Elaine Smith), virtually being jilted at the altar. Shane also famously had a punch up with Guy Pearce's character Mike Young over Jane Harris' affections.

CAREER SINCE

Like Guy Pearce, Peter took his talents to other parts of the world after leaving *Neighbours*. Unlike Guy, however, who skipped between LA and Australia, Peter sought his overseas experience in Britain, with equal success. And like most actors, not all of the film and TV projects in which Peter has appeared have been creatively or commercially successful.

He too has mixed excellent roles, such as in *Flying Doctors*, *Halifax f.p.*, *Day Of The Roses* and *White Collar Blue* with less popular ones such as *Relic Hunter*, *Flipper*, *Time Trax* and *Hotel de Love*.

But his choices when working out of London have invariably been spot on – DI Peter Cavanaugh in *The Bill*, Dr Cyril Scissors in *Cardiac Arrest*, Cameron Roberts in *Queer As Folk* and the lead in the tele-movie *Deceit*.

Most recently in Australia, he gave a stunning performance in the Lindy Chamberlain mini-series *Through My Eyes*, which obviously caught a few other eyes as well – he has since signed a three-film deal with an LA production company.

Peter's real love life has also taken an enviable turn — he is married to stunning and talented actress Miranda Otto (*The Well*, *Lord of The Rings*).

Alan Dale

NEIGHBOURS CHARACTER: JIM ROBINSON

Alan played one of the founding characters in *Neighbours*: Jim Robinson, head of the Robinson family. An architect, poor Jim saw his wife Anne die while giving birth to their youngest child Lucy.

That made him compassionate towards younger people, but blinded him in the love stakes, often choosing inappropriate (and sometimes much younger) partners – such as the callous Fiona Hartman (Suzanne Dudley), who left poor Jim dying of a heart attack on his lounge room floor while she rushed to the bank to retrieve his assets. In real life, Alan Dale has proven to be a much much luckier man.

CAREER SINCE

Alan Dale has been a revelation since *Neighbours*, proving you're never too old to finally crack the big time, if you have talent. After leaving the show, middle-aged Alan and his family (he is married to former Miss Australia Tracey Pearson) moved to LA, where he grafted away before finally winning guest roles in a slate of key US television shows including *The X-Files*, *ER*, *The Practice*, *24*, *NCIS* and *The West Wing*, not to mention two Star Trek films.

His most recent long-running role has been as Caleb Nichol in the hit series *The OC*. One interesting aspect of Alan's success in America has been his success at playing senior American politicians – in *24* he was the ambitious vice-president who tried to unseat President Palmer, and he was in a similar situation again in *The West Wing*, as Secretary of Commerce.

QUOTABLE

"At the time, getting the role on *Neighbours* saved my life (financially) and my acting career, and I still feel very grateful for that. Over the years there were trials, however, and by the time I left the show, both the production company and I were pleased to see the back of each other.

"But looking back now, I feel a great fondness for the show and the friends I made making it. I am proud to have been one of the original members of the *Neighbours* cast, and to have been part of something that has turned out to be so momentous in terms of Australian television history."

ABOVE: Kylie Minogue in London at the premiere of animated film *The Magic Roundabout* in 2005.

Kylie Minogue

NEIGHBOURS CHARACTER: CHARLENE ROBINSON

It's hard to believe it, looking at Kylie now, but she was TV soap's first tomboy. Teenager Charlene was a mechanic, and preferred overalls to short skirts. Nor was she averse to a little physicality, despite her diminutive size – fans will remember she socked future husband Scott (Jason Donovan) when he made his first move on her.

Although she and Scott, moved to Brisbane to live in 1988 she remains one of *Neighbours*' most enduringly popular characters, and her wedding to Scott the show's most memorable moment.

CAREER SINCE

Kylie is indisputably the biggest star to have emerged from *Neighbours*, and while the popularity of Charlene both in Australia and Britain obviously helped kick-start her music career, her talent, savvy, ageless beauty (and sex appeal), work ethic, and that uniquely Kylie charisma have done the rest. With 39 hit singles and nine albums (plus a greatest hits double album) in Australia, Europe and Britain, she is alongside

Madonna as the only female artist to have No.1 hits in three decades.

Kylie's hits include *Locomotion*, *I Should Be So Lucky*, *Hand On Your Heart*, *The Devil You Know*, *Spinning Around*, *On A Night Like This*, *Can't Get You Out Of My Head*, *Come Into My World*, *Slow* and *Chocolate*.

Even more famously, Kylie's four world tours, including her latest Showgirls tour, which began in Scotland, have been hugely successful, utilising her flair for fashion (she also promotes the top-selling lingerie line Love Kylie) and performance in staging event-type masterpieces. And who can forget her performance at the closing ceremony for the Sydney Olympic Games (seen by four billion people worldwide)?

Kylie has the knack of appealing to males and females, regardless of sexual orientation, and she famously always appears to be "up", never having a bad word for anyone. Her fans include Robbie Williams, Michael Parkinson, Dame Edna Everage, Alice Cooper and Madonna (who once performed in a Kylie T-shirt).

ABOVE: Jason Donovan addresses the media at an actors' strike in Melbourne in 2003.

Although her acting – she has had small roles in the likes of *Cut*, *Street Fighter* and *Moulin Rouge* – has taken a backseat to music, she retains an ambition in films. But with a zillion awards and accolades already in her kitbag, plus that can-do Charlene attitude, Kylie's future remains truly indefinable.

"I loved playing Charlene. She was feisty and rebellious and, as is the nature of soap opera, full of surprises. With her determination to be a car mechanic she became something of a high-school feminist figure. Fresh out of school and fairly determined myself, she was easy to relate to. With distance from those days I can now appreciate them much more ... *Neighbours* and its environment was an incredible learning curve. (The work ethic) also paved the way for easy assimilation into the (Stock, Aitken, Waterman) "hit factory" – in soap it isn't about you, it's about teamwork."
– From *Kylie: La La La*

Jason Donovan

NEIGHBOURS CHARACTER: SCOTT ROBINSON

Scott was Jim's (Alan Dale's) son and the grandson of Helen Daniels (Anne Haddy). He was a journalist and pursued Charlene (also his then girlfriend in real life) with a passion that endeared him to young lovers everywhere.

When they married it was not only the biggest event on the show, but in the media as well, making all the papers, magazines and evening TV news services.

CAREER SINCE

Jason has seen a lot in both his career and his personal life, tasting the absolute highs – a Logie as Australia's most popular young actor, starring in a hit West End production of *Joseph and The Technicolour Dreamcoat*, and sharing the No.1 UK and Australian hit record *Especially For You* with Kylie; to the absolute lows – such as making headlines after experiencing some personal problems in the mid-90s.

But these days, Jason's career is going from strength

to strength with one of the main catalysts being, his solid relationship with partner Angie Malloch.

The subsequent birth of their children Jemma (in 2000) and Zac (2001), plus the tireless support of his father, actor Terence Donovan, saw Jason reinvent himself as a responsible and reliable father and performer.

He has made a number of not-so-successful movies (*Rough Diamonds*, *Tempe Tip*, *Horse Play* and *Ned*) since leaving *Neighbours*, but like fellow cast members Guy Pearce, Peter O'Brien and Craig McLachlan, Jason has been much luckier on the stage, with hit British seasons of *Joseph*, The *Rocky Horror Picture Show* and, most recently, *Chitty Chitty Bang Bang*.

Only his once-stellar music career, which included nine solo top 10 UK hits and a multi-million selling album (*Ten Good Reasons*), has failed to regain impetus.

But his TV and film career is definitely back on track, thanks largely to his inspired casting as ruthless and charismatic lawyer Richard Savage in the ABC's critically acclaimed medical drama series *MDA*. He followed that up with the lead in the tele-movie *Loot*, and is being sought for numerous other projects.

QUOTABLE
"It was two weeks after I left school (when he joined the cast). I was Scott Robinson, launching *Neighbours*. I was a kind of good-looking, young, bright, fresh-faced, cheesy young guy, and we came in going, Wow – here's a cheque for $500 a week! Free cab vouchers ... you get treated like royalty. It's just a new world full of wonderful riches and I grasped the opportunities while they were there. Yeah – lucky man, definitely lucky, lucky, lucky ... I should be so lucky!"— *Australian Story*, ABC

Radha Mitchell

NEIGHBOURS CHARACTER: CATHERINE O'BRIEN

Before coming aboard as Catherine, Sarah Beaumont's (Nicola Charles) earth child sister, for a good chunk of 1996-97, Radha had earlier made a brief appearance as Cassandra Rushmore in 1994.

Catherine, however, was a regular, working in the coffee shop and helping out at the Wilderness Foundation. In fact she was passionate about everything, and she starred in an infamous moment when caught kissing Darren Stark (Scott Major), who was going with Libby (Kym Valentine) at the time.

CAREER SINCE

While *Neighbours* was hardly the launching pad for Radha's stellar career, making a brief appearance as Cassandra Rushmore while still a teenager first brought her to the casting department's attention.

A few years later, she was offered the much meatier role of Catherine O'Brien. Her two years on the show also coincided with her breakthrough film role in the small-budget, but critically acclaimed, *Love And Other Catastrophes*.

A slew of films followed, some forgettable such as *High Art*, *Sleeping Beauties* and *Kick*, but once she relocated to LA in the late 1990s her career took off. Her breakthrough film was probably *Pitch Black* (with Vin Diesel in 2000), while *Phone Booth* (2002, with Colin Farrell and Katie Holmes) cemented her place in Hollywood.

Since then, she has played the mother of the kidnapped child in the big-budget *Man On Fire* (with Denzil Washington), and opposite Johnny Depp in *Finding Neverland* (2004). She also caught the eye of filmmaker Woody Allen, who chose her to star in his latest film *Melinda and Melinda*, which was released in 2005.

QUOTABLE

"I used to be ashamed (of being on *Neighbours*) and tried to hide it, but now I'm proud of it ... I guess it was like being at school, and I did learn quite a lot." – *RedHot* magazine.

Kimberley Davies

NEIGHBOURS CHARACTER: ANNALISE HARTMAN

When the gorgeous Annalise arrived in Ramsay Street male fans couldn't believe it when she set her sights on the much older Lou Carpenter (Tom Oliver). But they were even more dumbstruck when the flirty hairdresser moved on to Mark Gottlieb (Bruce Samazan), only to have him jilt her at the altar and choose the priesthood instead. Were the scriptwriters making some sort of statement?

Nonetheless, Annalise's return to the series for the landmark 20th year of *Neighbours* has been the catalyst for re-introducing a swag of past characters (and stars). A budding poet, who also set up her own production company, Annalise returned in 2005 to complete a documentary on past and present residents of Ramsay Street.

SINCE NEIGHBOURS

With her stunning looks, Kimberley has been able to juggle modeling with her acting career. She was the poster girl for Macleans Toothpaste and did a major commercial for Tim Tams before she moved to LA to try her luck.

She's been in a string of movies and American mini-series (a remake of *South Pacific*, *Psycho Beach Party*, *Storm Catcher*, et al) before she finally found a niche as the stunning guest star on some of America's top TV shows – *Ally McBeal*, *Profiler*, *Spin City* and, most notably, *Friends*. Married to Doctor Jason Harvey, these days Kimberley juggles acting with bringing up her two children, Isabella and Josh.

SAYS KIMBERLEY OF NEIGHBOURS

"It's amazing when you realise the show is 20 years old and still going strong. It was a wonderful time of my life, and a great learning experience. With its exposure in Britain, the show provided the all-important stepping stone for successfully launching so many young Australians on the international scene. I'm so looking forward to coming home (to the show in 2005)." — *Herald Sun*

TOP: Radha Mitchell starring opposite Woody Allen in his film *Melinda and Melinda*. **MIDDLE:** Kimberley Davies in Melbourne during the Grand Prix.

149

Kylie Minogue opens her fourth worldwide tour – Showgirl.

Mark Little

NEIGHBOURS CHARACTER: JOE MANGEL

Joe epitomised the easy-going, boisterous-but-likeable Aussie bloke, and arrived in Ramsay Street with his young son Toby. He famously, and imaginatively, married Harold's daughter Kerry (Linda Hartley) in the Butterfly Enclosure of Melbourne Zoo.

Kerry died some time later while protesting against duck shooters. Joe later married Paul Robinson's (Stefan Dennis's) receptionist Melanie Pearson (Lucinda Cowden).

CAREER SINCE

While many *Neighbours* cast members make the traditional Christmas holiday trek to Britain to star in pantomimes, Mark Little went one better after his 1991 stint in *Snow White*: he made a lasting career for himself (as has Peter O'Brien and Jesse Spencer) in the UK.

His first major gig was as presenter of *The Big Breakfast* on Channel 4, but he has also since worked extensively (and successfully) throughout Britain as a stand-up comic (his shows at the Edinburgh Fringe have included *Mark Little Sucks*, *Psychobubble* and *Spontaneous Combustion*), and as a writer, narrator and presenter (for both TV and radio).

In 1999-2000, he wowed public and critics alike with an 18-month West End run of the hit one-man show *Defending The Caveman*, for which he later won the Laurence Olivier Award for Best Entertainment. He has since won further plaudits for his starring role (wearing high heels) as expatriate Aussie gay entertainer Leigh Bowery in both the West End and touring productions of the hit show *Taboo*.

Mark brought his family back to Australia for his 20th anniversary stint in *Neighbours*.

QUOTABLE

"It's only when you return you realise how much you really miss the place. Even British hits like *Coronation Street* and *Eastenders* screen there four nights a week, *Neighbours* runs five nights a week." – Little quoted in the *Herald Sun* upon his return to Ramsay Street for the 20th year celebrations.

Did you Know?

In a sly reference to the show's past successes, when Delta Goodrem's character, Nina Tucker, finally showed her talent by singing Born to Try in front of an audience, Toadie confidentally declared that Nina might well be "the next Kylie".

Craig McLachlan

NEIGHBOURS CHARACTER: HENRY RAMSAY

Henry was Charlene's (Kylie Minogue's) brother and, not surprisingly, the bloke's bloke when he arrived in Ramsay Street. He was always ready with a smile and a joke and capable of charming his way out of any situation, particularly with the girls. On the other side of the coin, Henry was easily led by others, a failing that resulted in him spending a little time in the slammer prior to his arrival in Erinsborough.

However, he eventually found his calling as a disc jockey, settled his roving eye on Bronwyn Davies (Rachel Friend) and they moved to New Zealand.

McLachlan won a bunch of Logies playing Henry, including Best New Talent, Most Popular Actor and the Gold Logie for Most Popular Personality.

CAREER SINCE

Life on and off screen briefly coincided when Craig married, for a short time, Rachel Friend, who played his girlfriend/wife in *Neighbours*. When he left the series, he moved directly to Australia's other popular TV soap, *Home And Away*, where he played the ongoing role of Grant Mitchell. Like a handful of his contemporaries from the early days of *Neighbours*, he then parlayed his British exposure and popularity by basing himself in London for a few years, appearing both on stage and on the small screen, the latter most notably as the co-lead in the spy series *Bugs*.

Like Peter O'Brien, and more recently Jason Donovan, Craig managed to establish his acting career both in Britain and Australia. He made a few movies and mini-series in Australia after *Neighbours*, and returned to Australia for guest roles in *Always Greener* and *McLeod's Daughters*. Any doubts about his acting versatility were spectacularly dispensed with by his performance in the lead role of Stuart Diver for the tele-movie *Heroes Mountain*, and, more recently, as Richard Chamberlain in the Lindy Chamberlain mini-series *Through My Eyes* (alongside fellow *Neighbours* alumnus Peter O'Brien).

Craig also starred as Danny in the arena production of the musical *Grease* in 1998 and 2005.

QUOTABLE

"I had no experience when I auditioned for *Neighbours* ... I was a 21-year-old kid, I just flirted with the producers like a madman. I thought, if I can make them fall in love with me and tell some funny stories, what I lack in technical ability they might think "Oh no, the kid's got something." – On *Enough Rope* with Andrew Denton.

OPPOSITE TOP: Mark Little, host of the TV show *Pants on Fire*.
LEFT: McLachlan in Australian telemovie, *Heroes Mountain*, as Stuart Diver.
RIGHT: Craig McLachlan as Richard Chamberlain in *Through My Eyes*.

Jesse Spencer

NEIGHBOURS CHARACTER: BILLY KENNEDY

The youngest of Dr Karl and Susan Kennedy's children, Billy was a sensitive young man, although he still managed to get into plenty of trouble with his mate Toadie (Ryan Moloney).

Although not as academically gifted as sister Libby (Kym Valentine), who became a journalist, he had a passion for furniture-making, which eventually enticed him away to work in the country. In a neat romantic twist for the series, his love, Anne Wilkinson (Brooke Satchwell), followed him there by transferring to the local university.

CAREER SINCE

Like many of the *Neighbours* cast, Jesse used his annual break from the show to travel to Britain and star in holiday-season pantomimes (*Peter Pan* and *Jack and the Beanstalk*) and parlayed his ever-increasing popularity into a huge post-*Neighbours* acting career.

Basing himself in London, he won leading roles in prestigious British tele-movies *Stranded* and *Death in Holy Orders*, then found favour in the US, with a continuing role in comic actor Hugh Laurie's American series *House*, followed up by a lead role in the film *Uptown Girls* opposite Brittany Murphy, Dakota Fanning and Heather Locklear.

He also made a trip back to Australia to star in the Australian film *Swimming Upstream*, alongside Geoffrey Rush and Judy Davis.

Daniel MacPherson

NEIGHBOURS CHARACTER: JOEL SAMUELS

It was no secret that with his good looks and sassy charm, Daniel was written into *Neighbours* to spice things up, and he certainly did that! From the moment he arrived in Ramsay Street, after befriending Mal Kennedy (Benjamin McNair) while he was on holidays in Queensland, he seemingly set every young woman's heart aflutter.

Dolly magazine readers voted Daniel The Most Dateable Man In Australia in 1998 and, the following year, he won the Logie for Most Popular New Male Talent. At various times on *Neighbours* Joel was involved with Anne Wilkinson, Hannah Martin, Sally Upton, Geri Hallet, Amy Greenwood, Natalie Rigby, Dee Bliss, Carrie Clarke and Flick Scully. He also managed to get Harold's blood pumping as his personal trainer.

Joel eventually returned to Queensland after qualifying as a marine biologist.

CAREER SINCE

Daniel left the show in 2001, having already set up a personal fan base in Britain through the popularity of *Neighbours*, plus his starring role in the Christmas panto *Aladdin*.

Soon after arrival he won a lead role in the West End production and then the touring company of *Godspell*, and followed that up with a continuing role in the hit TV crime series *The Bill*, playing PC Cameron Tait.

He left the series in early 2004 to star opposite Edward Woodward in the 14th-century play *The Mysteries*, spectacularly staged in Canterbury Cathedral.

At the end of the year he returned to Australia after being offered the host role in Network Ten's reality/variety show *The X Factor*.

LEFT: Jesse Spencer in *Swimming Upstream*. **RIGHT:** Daniel MacPherson at the 2005 MTV Awards. **FAR RIGHT:** Nathan Phillips with Chloe Maxwell in *Under the Radar*.

Nathan Phillips

NEIGHBOURS CHARACTER: JOHN "TEABAG" TEASDALE

Teabag was, for a time, *Neighbours*' resident bad boy, despite possessing ruggedly handsome looks.

He was a BMX fanatic who met a bunch of the Ramsay Street kids at the BMX track on Harold's allotment. He led Tad (Jonathon Dutton) and Paul (Jansen Spencer) astray, and then took a fancy to young Hannah (Rebecca Ritters). He was nothing but trouble, and when the boys turned on him, he harassed Madge and then wrecked the BMX track.

The boys also discovered he was responsible for a number of local break-ins. Even the bike he gave Hannah turned out to be stolen.

CAREER SINCE

Nathan went straight from his role in *Neighbours* into feature films, most notably his acclaimed performance in the AFI-nominated flick *Australian Rules*. He followed that up with a working trip to LA to make American movie connections, won a role in the martial arts action flick *Warriors Of Virtue*. Upon his return to Australia, he garnered lead roles in a string of films – the comedy *Takeaway* (opposite Vince Colosimo and Rose Byrne), *One Perfect Day* (with Dan Spielman, Kerry Armstrong, Leeanna Wallsman and Abbie Cornish) and *Under The Radar* (with Cloe Maxwell and Steady Eddy).

QUOTABLE

"I still get recognised as Teabag around Melbourne, but mostly by my mates who yell it out in the most embarrassing places and start to scream, and ask for my autograph ... it gets me attention I don't always want. But it is funny." – *MovieHole*.

The Last Word

Not every young aspiring actor who enters *Neighbours*, of course, emerges a fully fledged international star. But it's a matter of talentand personal expectations.

Back in the 1980s, Matt Stevenson played the dastardly Skinner, who abducted a child from Ramsay Street. These days he works as manager of a call centre, with nothing but good memories of the show.

"I still get recognised as Skinner. Last year, I was travelling on a train in Melbourne and I signed 40 autographs," he says.

"It's amazing how revered I am in other walks of life. Being in *Neighbours* has done me nothing but favours." ●

Street Party

Neighbours fans know the way to their mecca, and they come from far and wide to sing their favourite hymns, contemplate plot-lines, and worship the demigods of Ramsay Street. By Mark Dapin

*7*he (unofficial) church of Harold Bishop meets to worship its god on Monday nights at the Elephant and Wheelbarrow in Fitzroy Street, St Kilda, a cavernous, faux English-style pub. Mock Tudor beams in the bar, bangers and mash on the menu and the curious juxtaposition of its name promise half-familiar good times to suntanned travellers from Hemel Hampstead and Penge.

Monday night is the Meet Your *Neighbours* trivia night, organised by George Josevski, Melbourne's backpacker king. Harold Bishop (actor Ian Smith) appears to the faithful every couple of months. No other church can promise its followers the chance to shake hands with their favorite deity.

Josevski has been running the trivia nights — and the Official *Neighbours* Ramsay Street Tour — since 1998, but only won official recognition — sanctification? — from the show's producers, Grundy, in 2003. He says Smith, the show's longest-serving actor, is the most popular star with the crowds, followed by Alan Fletcher, then Ryan Moloney. British backpackers love to see people who were on TV when they were at school.

"Madge was very popular," says Josevski, then adds, in hushed reverence: "She died on the show a few years ago."

I'm sorry.

"Don't be sorry," he says. "It's only a show."

There are about 300 people in the bar at the Elephant and Wheelbarrow, three-quarters of them women, almost all from the UK. They have just started drinking, but they are swaying and screaming, whooping and yelling, waving and singing. Harold is not present tonight — except in spirit — but they cannot believe they are in the same room as demigod Alan Fletcher.

"Karl is a legend! Karl is a legend!" they sing, religiously, like a castrato soccer crowd. "Tra-la-la-la!"

He is here with Natalie Bassingthwaighte, who plays Izzy Hoyland, and Blair McDonough, who stepped out of *Big Brother* and into the soap. Any move or word from Fletcher or Bassingthwaighte prompts some kind of roar from the assembled backpackers.

PREVIOUS PAGE: *Neighbours* fans cheer on their favourite cast members.
PREVIOUS PAGE, INSET: The Official *Neighbours* Ramsay Street Tour Bus.

Not obsessed
Just dedicated

OPPOSITE: Enthusiastic patrons queue up outside the Elephant and Wheelbarrow for the Meet Your Neighbours trivia night. **LEFT:** A fan clarifies her position. "There's a mixture of embarrassment and enthusiasm", says travel consultant Mark Pearle. **ABOVE:** Fans worshipping at the church of Harold Bishop shake hands with the great man.

"Doctor Karl," asks Natasha, "how long is your stethoscope?" (Lewd roar, hilarity, baboon calls, seaside pantomime noises.)

Did you know?

The most popular destinations for residents leaving Ramsay Street are, in order:

1 Going to live "in the country".

2 Going to Darwin, usually to work in the Darwin Lassiters.

3 Moving to Queensland.

4 Going to work or study in the United Kingdom.

5 Leaving (often to an undisclosed location) to be with a sick relative.

CLOCKWISE FROM BOTTOM LEFT: Fans get up close to one of the show's favourite characters, Alan Fletcher, Ramsay Street's Doctor Karl; the crowd scrambles for a shot of their favourite *Neighbours* stars at the Meet Your Neighbours trivia night; Alan Fletcher plays up to the adoring crowd; Natalie Bassingthwaighte sings.

Fletcher acknowledges the crowd gracefully and gratefully. (Ecstatic roar.)

Megan from Wales asks him a question: "Have you ever seen another cast member naked?" (Lewd roar.)

Someone else from Wales demands of Bassingthwaighte: "What's the secret recipe to the chocolates you keep making that men all love?"

"Do the men all love it?" asks Bassingthwaighte. (Lewd roar.)

"I don't know," she says. "They haven't tasted it yet. There's no secret recipe, it's just how to make it that — that's the secret." (A roar.)

The next backpacker to speak is introduced as "Natasha from Chesh-eyre". (Roar of regional recognition.)

"Dr Karl," asks Natasha, "how long is your stethoscope?" (Lewd roar, hilarity, baboon calls, seaside pantomime noises.)

"Well," says Fletcher. "I can tell you that my stethoscope (wild, whooping roar) is long enough (strangled screams) to go all the way to your heart." (Terrifying, fat-auntie-style 'Aaaaaaaaaaaaaaaaaaah!' roar.)

After the question-and-answer session, the *Neighbours* stars step down from the stage and set out to meet every single paying guest. The familiar theme music strikes up, but the crowd comes in too fast with, "Naaaaaaa-aaaaaaay-baaaaaaaaaaaars! Eveybody needs good naaaaaaaaaaaay-baaaaaaaaaa-aaaaars!"

"Wait until the song starts," cautions tonight's MC, Josevski.

"Naaay-baaars!" they sing, "Everybody needs good naaaaaaaay-baaars! That's when good naaaaaaay-baaars become good friends!"

Unfortunately, nobody seems to know any other words, and the chorus degenerates into chaos, until some misguided diehards come back in for, "We can find the perfect plaaaaaaaaaaaaaaaaaaan!"

It should, of course, be, "We can find the perfect bleeeeeeeeeeeeeend!"

Hugs and whispers

While a $200-prize trivia quiz carries on in the background, each woman in the audience has her picture taken kissing or hugging Fletcher. They whisper in his ear. What on earth are they saying?

"They ask what your character's up to on the show," says Fletcher, "and they pass judgement on that: 'You shouldn't be leaving (on-screen wife) Susan', and that sort of thing."

The *Neighbours* stars are watched over by minders who follow them everywhere. When Fletcher goes to the toilet, two heavies flank his cubicle to make sure over zealous fans don't mob him.

Most of the time, however, the audience is passive and delighted, buoyant inside its TV dream. I am told the only trouble comes from Australians, who occasionally shout inappropriate comments at the female stars, and try to pinch their butts.

But how many Aussies come here?

"Okay..." says minder Annette Fascelli, "...about two a fortnight. And they're usually with friends who have come over from England."

Josevski is encouraging a singing contest. Entrants can perform anything they like as long as it's the *Neighbours* theme tune, a football song, or their national anthem. The competition opens with a fantastically terrible God Save the Queen, followed by an even worse *Neighbours*. The crowd cheers the contestants, just to shut them up.

Every great religion has its mecca, and most worshippers at the (unofficial) Church of the Most Blessed Harold, Bishop of Bishops, have already been to the real Ramsay Street, quiet close of half-a-dozen houses in Melbourne's comfortable, suburban Vermont South. Nothing happens in Vermont South. About half

A photo of a Neighbours star is a prize photo to take home. "This is the Harbour... This is Ayers Rock... 'Oh my God! You've got a photo of Dr Karl!"

of the suburb is a bushland reserve. It does not even have a Big Thing, like a giant concrete koala, to attract and disappoint travellers.

If there was a Big Thing in Vermont South, however, it would be a Big Harold, and the Big Harold would be the most photographed Big Thing in Australia.

Since the show first achieved its fantastic popularity in the UK in the late-1980s (a peak of 20 million viewers in 1988 — the year after Scott and Charlene's wedding), British tourists have poured into Vermont South, gleefully taking photographs of themselves standing outside Harold's house, with or without their trousers.

This was before Ramsay Street tourism was organised, regulated and taken under the patronage of Josevski. Official *Neighbours* tourists don't get any more personal with Harold's letterbox than pretending to post letters.

There are two Ramsay Streets in Melbourne: one is in Burwood, the other in Brighton. Josevki used to ferry backpackers there to have their photographs taken.

"The street sign in Ramsay Street, Brighton, was three or four houses down from Shane Warne's house," says Josevki. "He was outside, thinking I was doing bus tours to his house!"

Today, he runs two tours a day. If the weather is fine and demand is robust, he will lay on a third visit. He estimates Vermont South sees 200–300 tourists a week, or about 15,000 a year.

"The Brits have to see Sydney Harbour," says Josevski. "They have to see Ayers Rock — they're the iconic photos they take — but a photo with a *Neighbours* star would probably be the prize photo to take home: 'This is the harbour ... This is Ayers Rock ... 'Oh my God! You've got a photo of Doctor Karl!'

FROM FAR LEFT: Ramsay Street's favourite rascal, Ryan Moloney, poses for the cameras. Patrons review their best shots on digital camera at the *Neighbours* trivia night. A fan arrives at the street, which hosts 200-300 tourists per day. A tourist waits patiently for a hero shot with the Ramsay Street sign. INSET: Stephen Lovatt hams it up with a fan at the trivia night.

The pilgrims

Mark Pearle, a travel consultant at St Kilda YHA, says 60–70 per cent of the YHA's business is British, and 40–50 per cent ask about the Ramsay Street tour. "Most of them come up with a bit of an embarrassed smile when they ask for it," he says. "It's like, 'Is it all right if I go on the *Neighbours* tours?' and they say it very quietly. There's a mixture of embarrassment and enthusiasm."

Peter Dodds, the show's producer for 10 years, says the British pilgrims have been "a phenomenon for some time". *Neighbours* represents "a funny, warm place, where everyone seems to have a bit more room to breathe than they might have in the UK".

Does anybody come to Melbourne just to see Ramsay Street?

"Yes," he says. "It's quite extraordinary, but by no means uncommon ... As soon as the show was sold into the UK, we knew there was a kind of fanatical feeling. We tried to keep the actual name of the street as quiet as we could ... but it just sort of got around."

These days, all the backpackers know where the "real" Ramsay Street is, but they still want their picture with the street sign. Luckily, Official *Neighbours*

Ramsay Street Tour guide Rick Forster has one he prepared earlier.

As the minibus pulls into the street, alongside a resident walking his dog, Forster produces a silver-painted PVC pipe topped with a Ramsay Street sign. He plunges it into a soft verge, and the streetscape is transformed.

Like so many TV stars, the street looks much smaller in real life. It's a tiny close, not the spacious streetscape you expect to see. Kind of like when you run into Tom Cruise without his platform soles.

Residents' cars turn in and out of the close, while Forster sustains his frenzied, fact-filled commentary. He stops outside one house and says: "When Joe Mangel moved down from Darwin with his son Toby, hooked up with Kerry Bishop, and adopted baby Sky, they were living here very happily together when tragedy nearly happened. Baby Sky was in the house by herself when the house caught on fire."

He grabs a breath. "Who do you think broke into the house and rescued baby Sky?"

"Bouncer the dog," replies somebody. Or everybody.

Fans take it in turns to pose with the Ramsay Street
sign on the site where the exterior locations are shot.

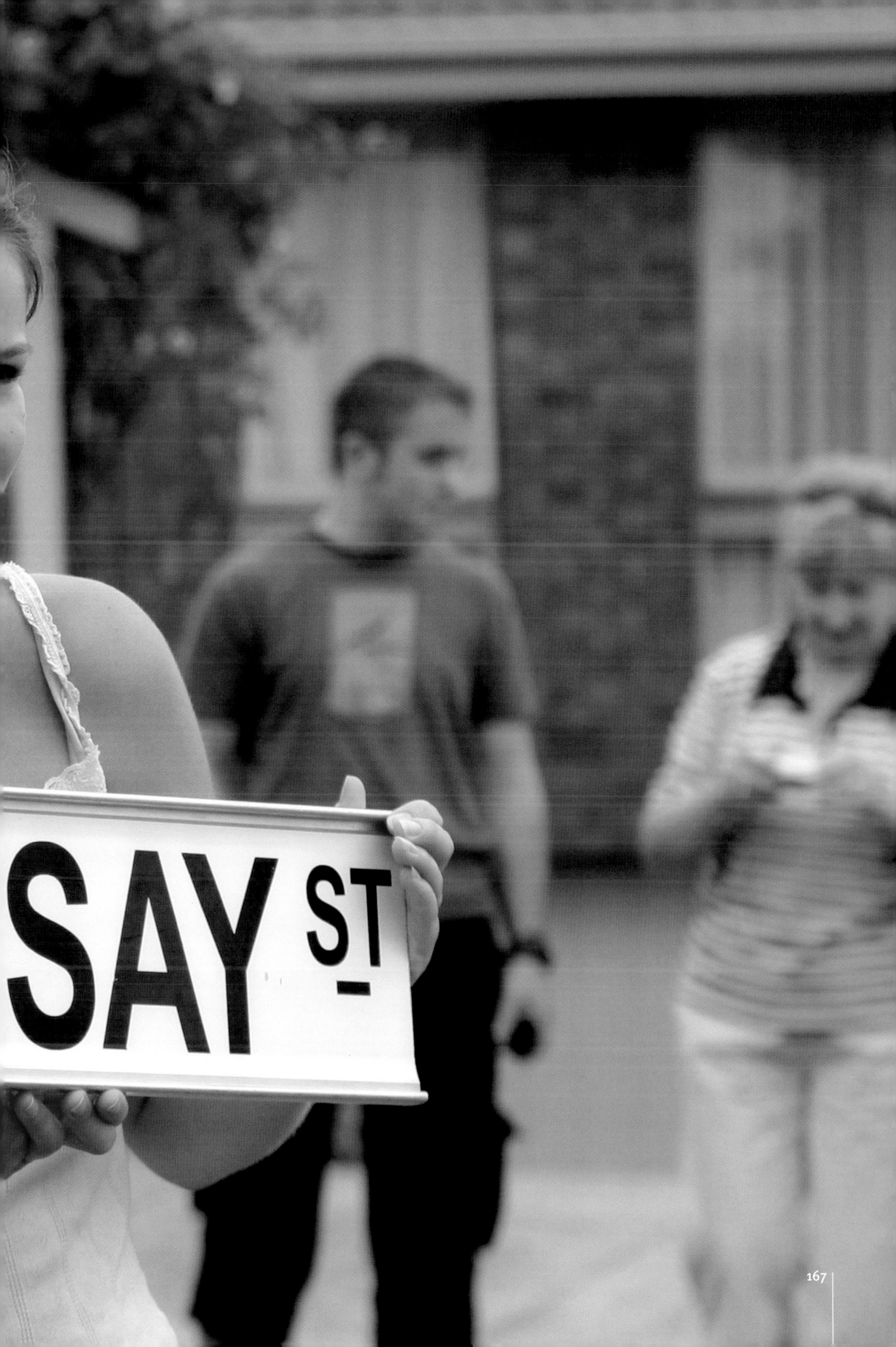
SAY ST

A vision of Dr Karl

Forster appears to know everything about *Neighbours*. When we leave Ramsay Street, we drive past Global Television in nearby Nunawading, where the interiors are filmed. Forster identifies vehicles in the car park, and searches vainly for Ian Smith's. Smith is not here but, magically, Alan Fletcher, who plays Dr Karl Kennedy, is just leaving the studio.

Fletcher offers a wave, and the bus pulses with loving admiration.

In the UK today, regular audiences are holding at six million, so not surprisingly Forster estimates about 90 per cent of his customers are British. He says he once had the president of the Canadian *Neighbours* fan club in the back of his bus. Although *Neighbours* is no longer actually screened in Canada, she has a friend in the UK send her tapes of the show, which she distributes among her 200 members.

Forster met his wife on the tour. Impressed by his phenomenal *Neighbours* knowledge, the Scottish working-holidaymaker went out for a drink with him afterwards.

"She bought me a pint, actually," he says, "and straight away that got her in my good books ... and before we knew it, I wasn't prepared to let the immigration department kick her out."

At the end of the tour, passengers can choose to be dropped off at the Melbourne Museum, where the Robinson family's kitchen rests in the Australia Gallery. The stuffed and mounted body of racehorse Phar Lap is the most popular attraction in the building but, says effusive customer-service officer Anthony McAleer: "For backpackers from the UK, this is Mecca."

Behind the kitchen is a reconstruction of the room where *Neighbours* actors and technicians used to wait between takes and the original studio door with an on air/in rehearsal sign mounted above.

"When the staff get a bit bored," says McAleer, "we tell kids *Neighbours* is being filmed behind the door."

It's a hands-on, walk-through installation.

"There must be tens of thousands of photographs of young British people standing in the kitchen," says Michael Reason, duty curator at the museum's history and technology department, "doing stupid things".

"They ask to see Kylie's (Charlene's) wedding dress, which was here for a while when we first opened, and unfortunately the guidebooks at the time wrote down that it was here permanently. We only had it here for about a year, but they still come in asking for it. It's actually in the permanent collection of the museum in Hobart."

There are "almost tears" says McAleer, when travellers realise the wedding dress is on the other side of Bass Strait.

Although No.26 Ramsay Street was home to the Robinsons, the Martins and, most recently, the Scullys, the kitchen has not changed much since 1985. It was repainted in 1997 because Philip's new wife Ruth didn't like the old colour scheme, and it finally burned down on the show so that Grundy could give it to the museum.

OPPOSITE: Fans photograph the bewildered students at the site of Erinsborough High.
OPPOSITE TOP: Fans at the Erinsborough High front gate. **RIGHT:** The *Neighbours* Official Tour Bus, on the job.

Neighbours trivia

Think you can match it with the experts? Test yourself with these brain teasers.

Who are the three most popular Neighbours characters?
Harold Bishop (Ian Smith), Doctor Karl Kennedy (Alan Fletcher) and Toadfish Rebecchi (Ryan Moloney).

As Daphne lay dying in hospital, what were her last words?
"I love you too, Clarkey".

When Todd was hit by a car and killed, why was he running across the road?
To tell Phoebe not to go through with her planned abortion.

Who was Bouncer's love interest?
Rosie, the sheepdog.

Alan Fletcher, who plays Dr Karl Kennedy, is just leaving the studio. Fletcher offers a wave, and the bus pulses with loving admiration.

ABOVE: The Robinson family's kitchen in the Australia Gallery at the Melbourne Museum.
RIGHT: The Melbourne Museum, home to the original kitchen of No.26 Ramsay Street.

The two-door shrine

"We get backpackers who come here for anything up to two hours," says McAleer. "They take photographs of themselves pretending to be cooking and doing the washing up, and when they open the fridge door ... that is like a shrine."

There is only one item in the Robinsons' fridge: a plaster model of Scott and Charlene's wedding cake.

"The museum put the exhibit here to recognise local television productions," says McAleer, "but what we discovered is that a lot of people from the UK actually believe that Melbourne is like what it is on *Neighbours*."

The exhibit has "polarised people", says Reason, "between those who said, 'Uh, what's that doing in a museum?' and those who thought it was wonderful."

A mob of local schoolchildren swarms into the kitchen, pulling on the fridge door, twisting round the sink taps, picking at the glued-down food jars.

"Everything in this kitchen appeared on *Neighbours* on TV," McAleer tells them.

"Even us?" asks a cheeky boy. McAleer smiles.

"The show is filming behind that door," he says, jokingly. "Give it a knock, and they'll let you in."

George Josevki keeps in close contact with Alan Shade, who, until recently, ran UK *Neighbours* fan site, www.erinsborough.com. Members of the site's forum formed groups according to their favorite characters. "The Max and Steph Group are going out to Australia at the end of the year," says Shade. "They've spoken to Carla Bonner, and some of them met up with her in the UK."

Shade, a librarian from Lewisham, loves the Ramsay Street tour. "The bus is completely kitted out," he says, "covered with *Neighbours* motifs. Seeing all the people looking at you driving up the motorway and then actually getting to Ramsay Street itself, is pretty amazing."

He went to trivia nights "six or seven times" when he was in Melbourne last year. They were "just crazy", he says. "When you're in the UK, *Neighbours* is big, but it's still got a bit of a daggy reputation – but going there, meeting Harold Bishop, just seeing how everyone went absolutely wild ... you'd think we were still in the Kylie/Jason era."

Shade has been watching *Neighbours* all his life. "The biggest soaps in the UK are shows like *East Enders*," he says. "It is quite depressing, and the storylines are quite bleak; there's hardly ever any

While Phar Lap is still the Melbourne Museum's most popular exhibit, the Robinson's kitchen is a "mecca" for British tourists.

characters on there that you actually like. Whereas, everyone on *Neighbours* is nice. Even when awful things are happening, it always works out in the end. I think people here like the fact that there's such a good community spirit in Erinsborough. You probably don't talk to your own neighbours, but you like watching people who get on really well with their neighbours."

What did he think of the real Melbourne?

"I was pretty much in *Neighbours* World most of the time," he says, "so it felt like I was in the show, anyway. I worked in the script department for a couple of weeks, watched them when they were story-lining and had a bit of a say. I really liked Melbourne; I thought it was pretty comparable. Everyone I met was really, really friendly. Everyone was willing to open their house to you."

But Ramsay Street is usually as sunny as Charlene's smile. It has only rained four times on the show, ever, and Shade visited Melbourne in the winter.

"It did rain most of the time," he admits. "It was pretty cold. So that was a bit different."

There are some things on this earth, like Melbourne's weather, that even The Most Blessed Harold cannot control. ●

RIGHT: The Most Blessed Harold, worshipped by followers at the *Neighbours* trivia night. **BOTTOM LEFT:** Fans wait patiently outside the Elephant and Wheelbarrow. **BOTTOM RIGHT:** The *Neighbours* bus, says Alan Shade from Erinsborough.com, is "completely kitted out".

Cast and crew celebrate the 500th episode at a *Neighbours* party.

The Neighbours Story

Year by Year

By Lorin Clarke

174

LEFT: An arial view of Ramsay Street as it was in the early days of *Neighbours*.
RIGHT: Mrs Mangel with her friend Eileen at the Erinsborough bowls club.

*N*eighbours' opening episodes immediately enmeshed viewers in the lives of the people on Ramsay Street. There were pre-wedding jitters, family secrets, questionable paternity, and a stripper named Daphne. Viewers met Des Clarke and Lorraine Kingham in the lead-up to their wedding.

Still hung over from his buck's night, Des answered the door to be confronted by a doubtful Lorraine and her parents, while behind him a stripper emerged from the bedroom to announce she'd found her watch. Lorraine, an increasingly reluctant bride, now had it confirmed Des was not the man for her and called off the wedding. Des was devastated and, craving company, defied protests from resident grump Max Ramsay and invited Daphne to move in.

Two doors down, Max was furious to find that his son Shane was falling for Daphne. Max's own troubles overtook him, though, when his wife, Maria, revealed that he was not the father of their other son, Danny. Max moved out. To make matters worse, Terry, the apprentice Maria hired to help in Max's plumbing business, turned out to be a woman. A woman who was immediately interested in Shane. Maria was having a romance of her own, with new man Richard Morrison. Danny refused to accept this relationship, and confronted Maria with a choice: it's Richard or me. Maria considered a difficult decision. She chose Richard and they both left town.

The air was thick with romance at the Robinson house, with Jim Robinson interested in Anna Rossi. Helen Daniels, usually the advisor in such matters, found herself tempted by the advances of Douglas, an art dealer interested in selling her art. Later, sadly, he left town having stolen all Helen's money. Julie met banker Philip Martin and began an affair with him, even though he had a family. She faced the consequences of this when Philip's wife, Loretta, turned up and attacked Julie with a knife. Philip wanted to leave the alcoholic Loretta, but he retreated home when his daughter, torn apart by her parents' unhappiness, attempted suicide.

Shane and Terry, now a couple, were shocked when Terry's ex turned up, having escaped from prison, and held her hostage. Terry's secret past, tainted by criminal activity and a husband nobody knew she had, killed her relationship with Shane, who couldn't continue to be with her, knowing what she had done. A day after breaking up with Shane, Terry accepted an offer to spend the evening with Shane's friend Paul. Later that same night, she accepted a much more surprising offer when Paul proposed. Paul and Terry were married in a ceremony that survived bomb threats, mysterious coded messages for Terry, and a tense period in which it seemed Paul had run off.

Then came Erinsborough's first murder. Terry realised the mysterious threats she had been receiving were from a dangerous criminal from her past. Desperate, she took matters into her own hands and shot him. Daphne was framed for the murder, but Paul worked out who the culprit was and confronted his wife. Terry shot him. He survived, but she was caught and slowly continued her downward spiral. She later killed herself in prison.

1985

1986

A surprising rumour was haunting Erinsborough at the start of 1986: A gorilla was apparently loose in Ramsay Street. Further investigations revealed that Clive Gibbons, who ran a gorilla-gram service, had moved into No.22. Clive later appeared unusually gifted when he performed an emergency tracheotomy on Lucy at the dining room table in front of the Robinsons. His secret was revealed: Clive was a qualified doctor.

Helen and Madge exacted revenge on Helen's art dealer, getting Helen's money back. The increasingly popular Daphne was going out with Shane, but turned down his proposal when she realised she preferred Des. In time, Des proposed. When the wedding day came, Daphne made a mistake that would cost her considerable heartache: She was late. Panicking, Des decided she wasn't coming, and left. Daphne was devastated. Shane saw Des and Daphne's break-up as an opportunity to prove that he was right for her. Soon, they were engaged.

Daphne's questionable timing meant she then had dinner with Des. Dinner was lovely and Daphne broke up with Shane. Mike, then just a kid working in the coffee shop, admitted his father was abusive and Daphne took him under her wing. Then Andrea arrived, claiming untruthfully that Des was the father of her son. When this was disproved, Des proposed to Daphne and she accepted.

One day, Scott saw someone breaking into the Ramsay house. He tackled the culprit, who punched him in the face. The intruder was revealed to be feisty Charlene, Madge's daughter. While Scott and Charlene fell for each other more or less immediately, Madge tried to reconcile with her family. Charlene's dad visited, slept with Madge, dumped her and shot off again. Madge's brother Tom arrived and drove her crazy. The coffee shop received countless complaints, meaning Mrs Mangel was in town, so No.32 now housed Madge's least-favorite nosey parker.

Zoe, Paul's assistant, fell pregnant to Jim, who proposed. Zoe refused and later had a miscarriage and left. Eventually even Shane approved of Daphne's wedding, which went without a hitch. On the way home, however, Shane crashed his car and killed Tom's girlfriend. At the scene, he sipped brandy to calm his nerves, but was later breath-tested and charged with manslaughter. The charges were dropped.

Mrs Mangel's granddaughter "Plain Jane Superbrain" arrived and fell for Mike, who asked her to the school dance. Helen and Daphne, utterly brilliant in that kind of crisis, transformed Jane, in one expert make-over, into a beautiful woman.

Charlene shocked Madge when she presented a baby that turned out to be Charlene's Dad's. Daphne contracted meningitis and Mike's ex-girlfriend, Nikki, returned to pose a brief, but dramatic, threat to Jane. Warren came briefly between Charlene and Scott. Nikki's mother Laura revealed that Helen's best friend had had an affair with Helen's late husband.

Paul, having put everyone briefly offside for suggesting they tear down Ramsay Street and erect a supermarket, began an affair with Susan Cole – Charlene's father's jilted lover – almost as soon as she rejected Clive's proposal. Jane and Shane got lost in the bush, making Mike jealous.

Finally, having dealt with their apparent infertility, Des and Daphne conceived a child.

FROM FAR LEFT: Cast members celebrate the first anniversary of *Neighbours*; cast from 1986; Scott and Charlene survey the charred remains of Charlene's caravan; the filming of a scene in Des and Daphne's kitchen.

*S*exual tension palpitated from the screen in 1987. Susan left Paul to marry Clive. She refused Paul's advances in the office, so he fired her but Clive was hurt and Susan left town. Her replacement at work was Gail. Gail and Paul had once had an affair when they were air stewards, but her ex-husband Jeremy turned up to woo her back. When he was killed in a car accident, Paul was all too happy to comfort Gail.

New girl Kelly, Charlene, Mark and Scott went to the beach and the boys' clothes were stolen, leaving them naked for all to see. Charlene, still fighting with Madge, moved into a caravan, but it exploded. Madge and Jim, much to Scott and Charlene's despair, wouldn't allow them to move in together. Scott decided to become a journalist so he started writing for the *Erinsborough News*. Shane left to travel Australia just as Madge's son Henry turned up from jail, much to Mrs Mangel's delight. Harold Bishop, an old flame of Madge's, came to town and opened a health-food shop.

Harold proposed to Madge, but reconsidered due to Madge's parenting problems with Charlene. Madge was furious with Harold, Harold was furious with Madge, and Charlene was furious with everyone. Sick to death of their parents, Scott and Charlene decided to get married. The famous wedding day arrived and it was fabulous. Scott and Charlene's feuding families were finally united.

Less romantically, Paul and Gail married at No.22 in order to seal a business deal. Despite not being in love, they found that being together brought out feelings

they hadn't experienced before. Jane became "Lassiters' Girl", but she hadn't lost her brains, so she agreed to help Scott with his exams. After spending a great deal of time together, things got the better of them and they kissed. Jane felt awful and left on a business trip, and Scott had to face the music alone.

Mike and Jane realised their careers were leading them in different directions and drifted apart, while Charlene soon forgave Scott. Scott's dad Jim was disappointed when the new lady in his life, Beverly, with whom he had many spirited arguments, was whisked away by her ex-husband. In one of the show's more unfortunate injuries, Harold broke both arms when he crashed the car on which Charlene had not yet fixed the brakes. Daphne and Des had their baby, James.

Des' sister and father arrived and Des had plenty of work ahead of him to ensure his parents got along. Scott was lost at sea for a time, but was found, to everyone's relief. He returned to find his exam results were not good enough to help him get into journalism.

1987

es' parents announced they were remarrying. Mrs Mangel, with her usual sensitivity, gave Malcom a couple of reasons to call it off, which he did. Harold became the anonymous *Erinsborough Times* agony aunt and was hugely popular. Mrs Mangel found out and secretly took up the column herself, advising John Worthington to propose to her. He found out and dumped her.

A series of dramas began with Madge winning a car in a raffle and Henry teaching her to drive. The lessons cut a fine line between comedy and drama, but ended when Madge knocked down a fire hydrant, sprayed everyone and promptly sold the car. Jim and Beverly married and Paul and Gail renewed their vows, but the day was marred by Katie and Todd Landers, Beverly's niece and nephew, going missing. They were found but refused to go home. In no time, they were living at No.26. Meanwhile, Scott suspected his boss was dishonest. When he reported him, the boss burnt the factory to the ground. Jim started work at Rob's garage.

Soon, a tragedy struck Erinsborough that made everything else fade into insignificance. Daphne had been comforting her dying father, but as Gail was driving her home, they had a terrible accident causing Daphne to fall into a coma. Des sat by her and told her how much he loved her. She stirred in her sleep, said, "I love you too, Clarkey", and died in his arms. Des was beside himself.

Mike, devastated by the death of the woman who changed his life, attacked the drivers of the other car. He faced assault charges when the men went to the police with horrible injuries, but Scott and Henry exposed the injuries as fakes. Harold, having successfully proposed to Madge, taken it back and re-proposed, then once

again called off the wedding. He had lost all his shares and couldn't afford it. So, who should turn up? His rival Lou Carpenter. There were flowers, fist-fights, and Madge threw a glass of water over them both in her driveway. Madge chose Harold and they finally married.

Nina, Paul's old flame, turned up with Amy, Paul's child, and Paul and Gail conceived triplets through IVF. After Daphne's death, Mike watched as Jane, the girl of his dreams, fell for Des, his guardian. Scott and Charlene returned from Brisbane in a bad way after Charlene kissed her driving instructor. They remembered how much they adored each other and moved on.

Des' babysitter Bronwyn got the boys talking. Mark had a brief affair with her, much to the disgust of Henry, who eventually won her over. Mark, teaching at Erinsborough High, befriended a girl whose father had abused her, just as Mike's had. When they were caught kissing, Mark was suspended from teaching and left town. Bronwyn's sister Sharon arrived, and the sisters experienced the singular pleasure of living with Mrs Mangel. Des and Jane eventually got together. Scott made the controversial discovery that Ramsay Street should have been called Robinson Street. It had been named as a result of a card game between Jack Ramsay and Old Grandfather Robinson in which Jack cheated. Todd and Katie changed the street sign and everyone was scandalised. The matter was settled in a card game that Charlene rigged. Henry won. Dan Ramsay bought Charlene a house in Brisbane and Charlene left Ramsay Street. Scott had to wait until he got a job there.

Sharon, who was given a cigarette and threw it in the bin, inadvertently set the Coffee Shop on fire and it blew up. Des was only just saved from the inferno by Harold. Beverly thought Jim didn't want a child, and attempted suicide. Mrs Mangel left to live with John Worthington in London. Jane became engaged to Mark, an American businessman. Todd ran away with bad boy Skinner, but returned in shock when Helen had a stroke.

1988

There was something of a changing of the guard in 1989. If viewers thought Beverly looked different on her return from Perth, it was because a new actress, Shauna O'Grady, was now playing the role. Henry, Jane, Gail, Des and Mike moved out and Ramsay Street met the Willis family.

Jane was taken aback when Mark's mother told her not to marry him. Rosemary also disapproved and had a fight with Jane. Rosemary tried to get Jane sacked from her job, but Jane got in first and resigned. She soon realised Mark wasn't for her after all, and called it off. Helen, now recovering from a stroke, returned to find everyone looking after her. This was a role reversal she wasn't happy with. Harold asked his daughter Kerry and granddaughter Sky to live with him, despite his disapproval of their hippy lifestyle. He approved even less when Joe Mangel became romantically involved with his daughter.

Paul found it hard to be around as much as Gail would have liked. Scott kissed Poppy, a girl at his work, but realised once again that Charlene was the girl for him. On his road trip, Mike had a bike accident that left a girl, Jenny Owens, paralysed. Jenny convinced Mike the accident wasn't his fault, and left town. Mike's problems were far from over as Des and Jane, at last, realised their mutual attraction and became engaged. Love was well and truly in the air at a double-engagement party they held with Joe Mangel and Kerry Bishop. Mike turned up and shouted his disapproval. He came around to the situation when Jane talked to him.

Only one of the happy couples, Kerry and Joe, made it to the altar. Not even the romance between Henry

and Bronwyn lasted long. Bronwyn accepted Henry's proposal, but called the wedding off. Des wasn't so lucky in love, either. When Mrs Mangel had a heart attack in London, Jane left to look after her, and was a long time coming back. Des went to London to persuade Jane to come home and marry him, but she had decided it was not to be. Des was devastated yet again. Mike left to care for his sick mother.

Katie and Todd's Dad turned up and demanded his kids back. Katie agreed to go, but Todd refused and said a tearful farewell to his faithful little sister. Lochy McLachlan met a ghost who turned out to be Lee. Lee wasted no time getting close to Matt, the boy who turned out to be Hilary's son. Things weren't getting any better for Paul and Gail. Paul caught Gail's father stealing parts from the garage. The father denied everything and left, but his car crashed and he died. Gail, still pregnant, left Paul and went to New Zealand.

The Willises arrived, with Cody seducing Todd away from his promise to his first girlfriend, Melissa, who was overseas. Nick came down with meningitis and Sharon broke up with him. Henry got a job on radio and was so terrible that callers phoned in with fake names, trying to make his show more interesting. Eventually, Henry got a job as a DJ in New Zealand and said a tearful on-air goodbye to everyone, especially Bronwyn.

Beverly, still yearning for a child, took on an infant who had been dumped by a depressed patient. Not only did the child – Rhys – nearly die of a chest infection, but his father demanded $1000 from Beverly, who was trying to hide the drama from a very concerned Jim. The year ended with Madge winning the lottery.

1989

adge and Harold spent their new money by going to Europe and – increasing the entertainment value of living in Ramsay Street – erecting a spa in their backyard and routinely skinny-dipping. Des, after a terrible couple of years, announced to everyone's relief that he had fallen in love with a widow and was moving. Doug Willis came to help set up the house for sale. He ended up buying it and moving in.

Todd had to face the music when Melissa returned from overseas to find him with Cody Willis. Each girl had been led to believe she was the only one, so they both dumped him. Melissa forgave him, though, but when he found out why (she had cheated overseas), he dumped her. Josh Anderson arrived in town and went out with Melissa. Todd was jealous so he woed Melissa back only to watch Josh get together with Cody. The star-crossed lovers worked it out when it became clear that Cody and Todd and Melissa and Josh were meant to be together.

Jim discovered Beverly was being bribed so he called the police. Rhys had to be returned. Lee left a miserable Matt, and Ramsay Street, forever. Bronwyn, finally seeing sense, left to marry Henry in New Zealand. Sharon followed her. Nick left, too, to go to a London art school.

As usual, when residents left, other people arrived. Gemma Ramsay turned up and refused to go out with anyone. She did have a false start with Ryan before realising she was attracted to Matt, who then forgot about Jill. Lochy McLachlan's Aunt, Dorothy Burke, arrived and became principal at Erinsborough High. There was another, more mysterious arrival in the form of Linda Giles, who

moved into Paul's and took on Gail's old job. Paul started out thinking Linda was a fabulous worker but changed his mind when she turned into a hopeless, vague shambles every now and then. Eventually, Paul discovered that Linda Giles was in fact two people. One Linda walked in on the other having a conversation with him. Twins Caroline and Christina Alessi — Christina absent-minded and Caroline brilliantly organised — had been placed in Erinsborough by a witness protection program that had them pretending to be one person. A stalker who had been chasing them after they witnessed a murder was caught just in time, and the sisters revealed their true identity.

In huge news for Ramsay Street residents, Beverly and Jim broke up, and Jim began stepping out with Caroline. Beverly then revealed she had finally become pregnant. She and Jim got back together, but Beverly had a miscarriage and they finally divorced. With the Robinson house in disarray, Todd was sent home to live with his mother but he ran away and returned to Cody. The couple escaped but had to return when Cody became very ill. Adam Willis, Cody's brother, started dating Caroline.

Joe officially adopted Kerry's daughter, Sky. Then, Kerry was accidentally shot when protesting duck shooting, and she and her unborn child were killed. Sky's father turned up and demanded Joe give Sky back, given he now wasn't married and so could not legally keep her. Melanie offered Joe her hand in marriage to save him, but Joe refused. Sky was taken away.

Paul returned from a trip overseas and announced his engagement to a woman named Isabella. Chrissy revealed Isabella was only interested in Paul for his Australian passport. Soon after, Paul and Chrissy got together. Jim was confronted by a man called Glen Donnelly, who claimed to be Jim's son from the Vietnam War.

FROM FAR LEFT: The 1990 residents of Ramsay Street; Joe Mangel and family; Harold Bishop, before disappearing from the rocks, presumed dead; Paul and Christina with baby Andrew; the 1991 cast, complete with Bouncer.

Joe, desperate, kidnapped Sky from Eric, her father. This spurred a custody battle, which Eric won. Joe was gutted, having fought so hard for Sky. Then Eric conceded Joe was a better father and Sky was home at last. Paul and Christina were finally married. Paul decided he wanted to have a child, and this time to do it properly. Chrissy soon became pregnant.

Melanie, aware of Joe's unhappiness, started trying to find him the perfect girlfriend. Joe had another brush with the law when he was framed for a hit and run accident. He was cleared and realised that Melanie was the woman for him. Melanie had moved on now, and was dating Simon Hunter. Madge had an operation on her famous voice, but it returned! Dorothy was shocked when her ex-husband, Colin, was released from prison and tried to make a fresh start.

In one of the show's most controversial subplots, Lucy found herself attracted to Glen and pursued him not knowing he was her half-brother. Their attraction got the better of them and they kissed. Their family discovered this secret and Glen and Lucy stopped their affair. Joe was cleaning the window at Lassiters and saw Colin in bed with Rosemary. Then Dorothy discovered she had breast cancer, but she had a mastectomy and recovered. Harold lost faith in God when a boy died on a scout trip he was leading. Bouncer was mistaken for a savage dog and almost put down.

Gemma started going out with Adam, who had broken up with Caroline. The couple soon left for Newcastle. Glen's ex-lover Karen arrived, claiming she was carrying his child. Glen decided this was his responsibility, and proposed to Karen. She accepted. Josh, who was living with the Robinsons, developed a crush on Lucy and started buying her expensive gifts.

Helen met up with her late husband's cousin, Michael, and found she had so much in common with him that she accepted his marriage proposal. Shockingly, the stripper at Helen's hen's night turned out to be none other than Josh, who was stripping for cash to afford more presents for Lucy.

Karen and Glen were about to be married when Karen admitted the baby wasn't Glen's and called it off. Simon, Melanie's new man, proposed and she broke Joe's heart by accepting. Madge advised Joe to move on and appear on a TV game-show called Dream Date. Melanie went along for support and was selected as the secret date. She disguised her voice, but Joe picked her anyway and they won a holiday together. One thing led to another and the town's next wedding was a notch on the belt of TV game shows.

Harold had a heart attack but recovered fairly quickly to tour Australia with Madge. Tragedy struck, however, when Harold disappeared, presumed dead. Madge left to grieve with Scott and Charlene. Gaby Willis moved home and her brother Brad was dragged home by his parents after getting into drug trouble. Paul got stuck in the bush with Chrissy's sister, Caroline, and things hotted up. Then Chrissy gave birth to Andrew.

Cody, studying in America, broke it off with Todd. Melanie and Joe went to be with Mrs Mangel in the UK when she had another heart attack. Lou Carpenter was arriving back in Erinsborough just as Madge was coming home. Glen, fixing the banner on the roof of The Waterhole, fell off and became paralysed.

1991

Glen broke it off with Gaby and left with Karen. Chrissy's cousin Marco worked out that Caroline and Paul had had an affair. Caroline left Erinsborough to prevent Christina having to find out. "Creepy Phoebe" was no longer quite so creepy and she found herself having to choose between Todd and Josh. She chose Todd, and an epic romance began. Not long afterwards, the pair decided to sleep together.

Lucy and Brad got together, but Beth arrived and confused Brad, who was trying to live with her without noticing she was his dream girl. Marco, Christina and Caroline's cousin, kissed Beth, however she wasn't interested. Pam was accused of murder, but her lawyer nephew Cameron arrived and sorted everything out.

Jill Wier arrived and set her sights on Doug. Marco Alessi's brother Rick turned up to start at Erinsborough High. Christina, who had so far been protected from revelations of her husband's affair, overheard Paul admitting to Helen that he and Caroline had slept together. She threw Paul out and refused to let him see Andrew. Lou, never one to let an opportunity pass him by, proposed to "single" Madge. She refused because of Harold. Gabby's new boutique, Gabrielle's, exploded.

Phoebe discovered she was pregnant. She wanted to keep the baby but everyone – including an anguished Todd – advised her she was too young. Phoebe was checking herself in at the clinic when Todd had a change of heart. Running to stop her, Todd dashed across the road and was hit by a car. He died. A grief-stricken Phoebe found solace in one thing: she had decided at the last minute to have the child. A montage of Todd was played over

1992

the closing credits. Todd's funeral took a dramatic turn when his father briefly took Helen hostage, but soon everyone was united in grief.

Gaby was dating Melanie's ex, Simon, and decided to "take it slowly", but Simon raped Gaby. When her family found out, he snuck out of town. Doug and Pam were losing the spark in their marriage. Jim and Pam grew closer and Doug enjoyed the attention of Jill. Lucy finally won Brad over and decided to move in, but when she was given a modelling contract, she dumped him and left Erinsborough to become a star. Christina went to Milan to sort things out with Caroline. Then she sorted things out with Paul and the couple left to run hotels in Hawaii. Todd's Dad, still crazy after the death of his son, tried to take Phoebe hostage, but Brad got in his way and was shot. As Brad recovered, Beth realised she was in love with him after all. She asked him to sleep with her so she could erase the mental scars left by her abusive stepfather. He happily obliged.

Marco and Rick Alessi discovered they had a sister and Julie now had another family member as well. Her stepson Michael arrived, and they didn't get on. Phoebe, visiting Todd's grave, met Stephen Gottlieb. Stephen was visiting his girlfriend's grave and he and Phoebe talked about grief. Doug and Jill had a one-night stand. Jill then threatened suicide if Doug didn't leave Pam. Meanwhile, Pam kissed Jim. After getting to know each other, Stephen and Phoebe got engaged.

Rick and Debbie won a competition to meet Michael Jackson in the UK. Marco and Helen arranged for the trip in secret. Once in London, Rick and Debbie made friends with a leukemia patient and gave their tickets away. As a result, they ended up on television and their parents watched in disbelief as they appeared in a broadcast from England. Marco left town chased by loan sharks. Madge, realising there wasn't much to keep her in Erinsborough, left to live with Charlene.

FROM FAR LEFT: The 1992 cast photo; Todd's casket being lowered into the ground; Lou and his younger girlfriend Annalise Hartman; Stephen and Phoebe pre-wedding; 1993 cast photo on set.

Beth and Hannah were rescued from a burning cottage which Michael was suspected of lighting. Michael was found guilty of seeking to harm Julie and was sent to a detention centre. Hope Gottlieb was born in time to make her mother's wedding to Stephen perfect. Dorothy and Toby moved with Dorothy's new man – the education inspector – to the country. Bouncer went with them.

Jim decided to leave Ramsay Street. The neighbours thought he shouldn't, so that they launched "Operation Jim", whereby they made Ramsay Street undesirable to prospective buyers. After many hilarious attempts at driving people away, the residents admitted to Jim that they loved him too much to let him go. He stayed. Lou had a crisis upon turning 50 and found a new girlfriend, the recently graduated Annalise. Brad bought Beth a friendship ring. She was delighted and Brad realised her happiness stemmed from her belief that it was an engagement ring. He couldn't tell her the truth and she started planning the wedding. Brad met Lou's daughter, the gorgeous Lauren, at the beach and they became very close. Eventually, they made love on the beach.

Jim was secretly dating Annalise's mother, Fiona. When he gave her Anne's earrings, Helen was so outraged she moved out. Jim collapsed of a heart attack. Fiona attempted to revive Jim, and was about to call emergency when she stopped. She left and immediately transferred Jim's all savings into her account and later "discovered" Jim's body in public. Once she was found out, she had already skipped town. She later died in a car accident. Helen moved back into No.26 and sorted through Jim's things. She found a

letter that revealed that Julie wasn't Jim's daughter, but the product of a rape. Julie tracked down her father's son, the only living relative, who tried to rape her. She returned home and told Philip she wanted a divorce.

On Brad and Beth's wedding day, Beth saw Brad and Lauren together and called it off. Later, a new family, the Lims, walked in on Brad and Lauren on the couch during a house inspection. The Lims moved in briefly, but Julie's relentless racism drove them away. Phoebe and Stephen's lodger tried to kidnap Hope, but when Stephen took revenge, he targeted the wrong guy. He beat up Wayne, Helen's nephew, who was then implicated in a gang murder, but was later cleared.

A gas leak in The Waterhole caused an explosion. Stephen lost the use of his legs and some of his memory. He recovered and he and Phoebe moved to Anson's Corner to start a record shop. Beth and Brad, who were trapped together in the building, reunited. Paul and Lucy Robinson returned for Helen's birthday. Phillip and Julie reconciled, so Gaby missed out on getting Phillip's job.

Cheryl Stark arrived and took Lou Carpenter's breath away. Due to family disapproval, however, they didn't marry. Lauren, depressed to see Brad and Beth back together, joined a religious cult and was almost raped by the leader. Lou rescued her. Brad and Beth got married and moved to Perth.

Cody arrived, now played by Peta Brady. Cheryl's kids, Danni and Brett, having run away from boarding school, walked in on Cheryl on the couch with Jack, Gaby's lover. Gaby, who was learning to fly under the tutelage of Jack, crashed a plane. She and Annalise were left stranded in the wreckage.

1993

Annalise and Gaby were rescued from the plane wreck. Annalise returned to live with Mark and Gaby left for a job in Italy. When Lauren Carpenter and Wayne Duncan both left Ramsay Street, Danni Stark arrived to fill the gap. Cody and Michael returned and Rick developed feelings for Cody.

Cody's sister Gaby arrived home, pregnant with her flying teacher's baby. Cheryl was also pregnant, but her pregnancy was complicated when Julie accidentally drove into her in her car during an argument about Danni and Michael's developing relationship. Cheryl was confined to hospital, but Julie escaped conviction. Danni, who had weathered the storm of a drug scandal to reveal she was diabetic, got together with Michael, much to everyone's fury.

Debbie Martin was concealing an eating disorder when she collapsed in a deb ball rehearsal. When her family found out, they sent her to a clinic. Later, Rosemary asked her to move in with her, which she did. Mrs Mangel's ex-husband Len turned up and tried to swindle Helen in a dodgy business deal, but Michael prevented it. Rick quit school to be with his Japanese teacher, who couldn't cope with his obsession and left town. Cody and Rick got back together, but Michael and Danni were pulled apart. Michael was sent off to school in the outback to hone his practical skills. The pair parted emotionally. Cheryl and Gaby gave birth on the same day, Cheryl to a girl and Gaby to a boy. Trouble started when both babies were named Shannon, but their mothers agreed to use their middle names, Louise and Zac.

Mark's mother died, and Mark's father, Dave came to town. Annalise developed her interest in poetry and met Elliot Patterson, a publisher. Dave provided a remedy for Helen's eye problem that got Helen into a lot of trouble when she found out it wasn't normal medicine. Possibly even stranger than Helen taking drugs, Pam was given a motorbike and went to a rally where she met Sam. Sam's grandmother Marlene had just bought Cheryl and Lou's house, which Madge had sold without telling them. They moved down the street and Marlene took over their place. Marlene turned out to be Cheryl's mum.

Mark's sister Ren came to town to baby-sit Lolly. Gaby's parenting was brought into question when Jack returned and became possessive of his son. The couple reached an understanding and they left for Lassiters in Darwin with the Willises and eventually got engaged. Cody stayed at Marlene's. Just before Debbie left for New York to join Rosemary, her parents' fighting got worse and Julie seemed to be losing it. Julie turned up to a murder mystery weekend attended by Philip and screamed at him. The next morning, her body was found, having fallen, jumped or been pushed from a tower. Debbie cleared Philip of suspicion by revealing that Julie had been drinking and fell. When Debbie left, Hannah and Philip found their loss even harder. Hannah was behaving strangely and Philip turned to alcohol. When Rick was away, "Stonefish" Rebecchi, new kid in town, kissed Cody in full view of a camera, much to Rick's subsequent disgust. The couple made up.

The Kennedys moved into the Willis' house and Brett fell for Libby, Mal and Danni got together and Hannah chased Billy relentlessly. Mal accidentally shot Lou in the leg. Bianca, a homeless girl, started working for Sam. The object of Sam's affections, Annalise, accepted a proposal from Mark.

Things got worse for Sam when, on a disastrous end-of-year holiday, Squirrel claimed her unborn child was his. On the same holiday, Danni and Mal went missing at sea and Mal returned to hear a rumor that Karl had once killed a patient. On his return home, Mal stood in the waiting room and "outed" his father for murdering a patient. Lou, who was suspected of cheating with a younger woman he'd been meeting, revealed she was his daughter. Mark, torn between Jesus and Annalise, chose the former and called the wedding off.

FROM FAR LEFT: The 1994 cast photo at Lassiters; Marlene Kratz and Lou Carpenter with the Stark family and Brett's bird, Dahl; Bruce Samazan as the very religious Mark Gottlieb; the hunks of Ramsay Street circa 1995; Helen Daniels marries Rueben; the Ramsay Street residents of 1995.

Annalise, jilted by Mark who decided religion was his life, turned to Sam, who had always loved her. When they got together, Mark realised he wanted Annalise back. He begged her to convert to his strictly religious lifestyle. She refused. Despite Cheryl chastising Lou for keeping his daughter, Ling Mai, a secret, it turned out Cheryl had a daughter of her own. The daughter turned up, on the run from the navy where she was in an abusive relationship with her boyfriend, who later arrived and tried to strangle Cheryl, before Lou stepped in.

Marlene took the homeless Bianca under her wing, but Bianca soon left. Philip started dating a woman called Molly who looked way too much like Julie for anyone else to be comfortable with it, and Hannah took matters into her own hands by poisoning Molly, who left swiftly afterwards. Philip then met Cody's friend Jen, who was much younger than him, but who moved in and was cautious with Hannah. Hannah finally got a boyfriend, Lance, by changing tack and not dressing up and being flirty.

Danni and Mal moved in together, but had trouble meeting the rent so Stonie moved in with them. Stonie was with Cody for a time, but she started liking her uni lecturer, Adrian. After turning Adrian down, her marks dropped and she eventually had to bring a restraining order against him. When Stonefish allowed his mother to move in, Danni and Mal fled, and Angie and Stonefish were alone at No.32. Stonefish's brother, Toadfish, soon moved in. He and Billy made instant friends and hilarity ensued. Billy was in love with Melissa and they got together and decided to have sex. Their parents tried to stop them, but they would not be put off. When the moment came, however, they decided they weren't ready.

Libby's boyfriend Rupert cheated on her. Mark found Lucy Robinson dancing at a nightclub having turned to drugs and alcohol

after her divorce. Mark told her about her sister Julie and set about saving her from herself. In the process, they decided they liked each other, but once again Mark couldn't do anything about it, so Julie left for New York. Ren, Mark's sister, was briefly enjoying a stint as a headstrong businesswoman, strutting about and driving everyone crazy, but she soon returned to her hippy ways and met Luke and they left for Japan. Helen met Rueben, a fan of her art. They fell in love but she found out he had a terminal illness. Helen reconciled him with his son, married him, and he died days later.

Mark's piety was becoming too intense for the neighbours to stand, particularly when he started believing he was indestructible and sticking his nose in everyone's business. When, almost inevitably, he fell off a roof, he awoke from a coma and decided not to be a priest. He left town to star in a cooking show. Annalise's sister Jo then arrived and she was so chirpy and over-helpful she that drove everyone crazy. When their father turned up and revealed he was a female impersonator, Annalise and Jo found it hard to take. Annalise had an affair with Stonefish, and they were discovered in bed by Sam and Angie. When in Africa, Susan confessed to Brett that she had killed her own mother through euthanasia and Karl never knew.

1995

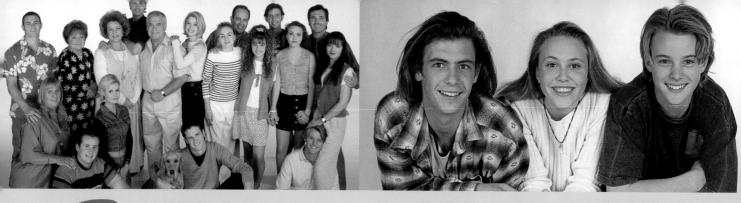

7here were some new careers this year, including that of successful romantic novelist Phillipa Martinez, who turned out to be Philip Martin. Daughter Debbie became a telephone psychic from her room. And none of the residents seemed surprised to find Clive James delivering the mail when he did a cameo for a day. A new radio show starred Lou and Marlene bickering. Plus there was now a resident genius in the surprising form of Toadfish, who shot off the charts on his IQ test.

Annalise moved out after her affair with Stonefish. Jen left Philip. Helen became a student. Brett had an affair with an older woman – Cheryl's golfing partner Judy. Susan was suspicious of Karl's relationship with a patient. Romance was blossoming between friends Cody and Sam. Danni started dating Rupert, Libby's ex-boyfriend. Sonny, who Libby met on the Internet, dumped her after she refused to have sex with him. Libby and Brett, best friends, decided to have sex to overcome their insecurities. Georgia came to stay with the Martins. Danni got a job in Sydney and Brett literally sailed away on a boat trip around the world.

Drugs were found in Mal and Sonny's new car and police waited to ambush the culprits who put it there. A shot was fired in the confusion and Cody, watching from the window, was shot and killed. Sam, ruined, drowned his sorrows until Cody appeared in a hallucination and assured him he would be all right. Danni returned with Ben, her fashionable, rich fiance. Hannah was delighted when Debbie returned, but Georgia was less keen to suddenly be sharing a room. Billy was having doubts about Melissa. When he kissed Georgia, Melissa walked in. Karl learned his father was not his real father after all. Luke discovered he had cancer and hid his treatment by shaving his head. Debbie read his confidential file and tried to help him. Danni ended her relationship with the rich designer after he lost his temper with her for making a mistake. Sam's modelling career

was so successful he was the prize in a dream date competition. The date was won by Catherine, a girl Stonefish was pursuing by pretending to be a vegetarian environmentalist.

Melissa's parents refused to allow a gay man to teach her but Billy and Melissa fought the decision, bringing them close again. Danni discovered Luke's secret battle with cancer and helped him through it. Cheryl was kidnapped in Ecuador. Lou went over and found her, returning to discover an affair she had while over there. They broke up and Lou left Ramsay Street. Sam left to be with Annalise in London. Jo married Rob and they left to America, but Jo returned when they broke up months later. Philip took in Casper, who Hannah took a liking to, but her attempts at romance were always thwarted. Libby got together with Darren Stark, fresh from prison. He bought Handy Sam's and settled into normal life. He was later cleared of blowing up the surgery, but was jailed for breaching parole.

Helen had another stroke, which Karl and Luke helped her through, hiring Ruth to rehabilitate her. Philip took a liking to Ruth. Toadfish's family left, but he stayed. Cheryl was run over by a car and Karl's treatment worsened her recovery. She died and the Starks blamed Karl, but soon turned on Lou, who returned to reveal he was the sole benefactor of Cheryl's will. Danni left soon afterwards and Karl quit medicine. Sarah Beaumont arrived, much to Toadfish's delight, although she was more concerned with avoiding Lord Steven Harrow, her famous fiance, and the media. Ruth's son Lance made friends with Hannah, and Ruth and Lance moved into the street. Libby broke up with Darren so he fixed the brakes on her car. Billy split from Melissa just in time to meet Ruth's daughter Anne. Luke left to be with sick Danni in Malaysia.

Then, lo and behold, Harold returned – all in one piece but with no memory at all – and was reunited with Madge. Lou helped Harold "remember" a version of the past in which Lou had been a true friend. But Harold recalled one of Lou's taunts and his memory returned. He and Madge started over and so did he and Lou, fighting constantly. Then Karl was faced with a dying Mal after an accident. It was up to him: could he save Mal's life or not?

1996

FROM FAR LEFT: The 1996 cast photo; Malcom, Libby and Billy Kennedy; *Neighbours* stars Moya O'Sullivan (Marlene Kratz), Bernard Curry (Luke Handley), Kym Valentine (Libby Kennedy) and Peta Brady (Cody Willis) together on set; the 1997 cast.

al recovered, much to Karl's relief, and Karl resumed work at the surgery. For a frightening moment it looked as though Toadfish might leave Erinsborough to live in the country, but Billy persuaded him to stay. Lou and Harold argued over whether a business should be a homeless shelter or a restaurant, and decided to bring their ideas together. The business failed and when it exploded Lou was suspected of having blown it up to collect the insurance. Darren kissed Catherine, infuriating Mal.

But there was also a whole lot of love in town. Harold and Madge renewed their vows. Lance walked in on Philip kissing Ruth in the kitchen and after a period of restraint, Phil and Ruth got together. Billy confessed his love to Anne and they got together, which was fine until Billy accidentally called Anne "Melissa".

Little else was going smoothly in Ramsay Street, with Libby refusing Darren's proposal, Debbie trying to break up Phil and Ruth, and one of Susan's students trying to tempt her from her marriage. Darren and Debbie spent more time together than strictly necessary and ended up dating. Mal left for England and Catherine surprised him by turning up at the airport to go with him. A newcomer, Ben, posed a threat to Billy when Anne decided she had a crush on him, but Ben refused her advances. Only after he introduced himself to Ruth did it become clear he was in fact Anne's brother, a child Ruth had adopted out when she was 15. It took a long time for the family to adjust.

Marlene appointed herself Karl's receptionist, causing him many headaches, culminating in Marlene competing with Sarah for receptionist of the year. Libby fell for Rohan, the blind man she did volunteer work for, but she was getting closer to Darren, causing Debbie to break up with him.

Things with Phil weren't working out, so Ruth prepared to move away again, but the kids changed her mind and Phil and Ruth got back together. Billy cottoned-on to the fact that his teacher, Lisa, was marking all his essays the same no matter how hard he tried, so he wrote "Lisa is a numbnut" in his next essay. She didn't notice and resigned. Harold and Madge decided to stay in Erinsborough rather than moving to Brisbane. Libby moved out after fighting with her father. Debbie bought a jukebox for the Coffee Shop against the wishes of Harold and Madge, who liked it even less after it electrocuted Harold. A protest by young patrons ended in Debbie quitting her job and starting up a rival business, the Lunch Cart.

Ben's sister Caitlin arrived and developed a crush on Billy. She soon moved on to James, leaving Billy a little bereft. Marlene went away on a three-month cruise, from which she is yet to return. Hannah and Madge reinstated the fight between the Ramsays and the Robinsons, but were talked around by Helen, who told them they should love each other. That night, Helen died in her sleep. Michael arrived and took Debbie home with him.

Paul McClain started lodging with Harold and Madge. The season ended with Billy getting into the swimming team and going to Sydney where Caitlin finally kissed him. Sarah got upset in Karl's surgery and they kissed, while Ben was involved in a car accident and there was a question mark as to whether he would survive.

1997

1998

en survived his accident, but other matters remained unresolved. Karl and Sarah tried to act normal in the face of many scenes where they were thrown inescapably together, but their attraction was obvious, especially when Karl saved Sarah from falling off a cliff to certain death. Ben's father turned up and tried to get between Ruth and Philip, eventually leaving town with Ben. Anne walked in on Billy and Caitlin kissing. Toadfish discovered Sarah's attraction to Karl and persuaded her to leave and live in a caravan park. Karl thought this was unfair to her and left to bring her back. The car broke down on the way home and they spent a night in a hotel.

Amy and Lance got together. Toadfish, a prankster from way back, caught a bout of community spirit and decided to save the school from being closed. Darren cheated on Libby with Sharon, so Libby finally dumped him. Darren left town and Libby was pleased to find his replacement at work was the handsome Drew Kirk. Libby and Drew became friends, though Libby believed Drew was in love with Sarah, who was, of course, in love with her father. Mal's triathlete friend Joel arrived to stay with the Kennedys, an invitation Mal had failed to tell his family about. Josh joined Caitlin's swimming team and the couple had many adventures and left their mark on Ramsay Street, literally. When they left, they painted 'Never 4Get Cait and Nick' on the road. Toadfish started working at the university radio station and soon had a fan base: Karen Oldman. Toadfish let Karen think Nick was him, so she would still like him when she saw the face behind the voice. When she worked it out, the real Toadfish found he had a girlfriend.

Madge and Harold were fighting with Lou, who was claiming a square metre of their land as his own. When Lou had a heart attack in the spa, the dispute dissolved. Billy told Toadfish that his father had stayed in a hotel rather than at home and Toadfish accidentally muttered something about Sarah. Billy demanded that Toadfish tell him what was going on.

A wedding was the perfect distraction. Phil and Ruth brought quite a crowd to their big day, which was made all the more enjoyable now that a lump in Ruth's breast had been cleared of being cancerous. Billy told Susan about Karl and Sarah. Susan slapped Karl in the face and told him to get out of the house. He left and the family was miserable until Libby went missing and Karl and Susan banded together. They agreed to try again. Libby was still furious with her dad and Drew was there for her, always. But she developed a thing for Mike, her university tutor, who had an ex-wife who was causing problems.

Lance's gambling habit turned into a problem and his dishonesty ruined his relationship with Amy. Anne's kindness to the elderly Lily Madigan, whose house was in danger of being bulldozed by developers, paid off when Lily passed away, leaving Anne her house. Hannah left to visit Claire in France. Tad Reeves, Toadfish's cousin, arrived to be reformed by Toadfish, who finally had to battle someone more troublesome than himself. Sally from Toadfish's work, meanwhile, had a brief affair with Joel, but left him to pursue Drew.

Amy and Lance looked like getting back together at the end of school summer break, and Anne slept with Billy for the first time at school camp, only to hear him talking it down the next morning. Upset, Anne left in tears, but the car got bogged by a river. Karl and Joel found her and tried to help, but the car rolled on top of Joel, crushing him. Anne went for help, but the rising water in the river was threatening Joel's breathing as he was trapped under the car. Would he survive?

FROM FAR LEFT: The 1998 cast photo taken at Lassiters; Doctor Karl does his best to prevent Joel drowning while Anne goes for help; *The Full Monty* team of Karl, Toadie, Drew, Joel and Billy; Kym Valentine, Nicola Charles and Brooke Satchwell celebrate the 3000th episode in 1999.

*J*ust as Karl was losing hope for Joel, help arrived and he was taken to hospital. Joel was devastated: his sporting career was over. Sally wasn't making matters any easier by pursuing Drew, but Drew knew his friend was suffering, and Sally left town. Anne was visited in hospital by Lily Madigan's nephew, who took Anne to court over who rightfully owned Lily's house. Anne won the case and she and Billy were reunited, but Bill's irrational jealousy eventually drove them apart. Amy and Lance had new romances for a while, but when they were single again, Lance was keen to reconnect. Toadfish had his hands full with Tad, who was making trouble everywhere, but soon had to grow up fast. He was diagnosed with a learning difficulty and after dealing with his parents' divorce, he learned he was adopted.

Things got unnecessarily raunchy at a fundraising evening when Karl, Harold, Toadfish, Drew, Billy and Joel were recruited to perform *The Full Monty*. Harold opted out, but the remaining boys were horrified when the lights came up at the wrong moment and they were all reported for indecent exposure. Libby's boyfriend Mike turned out to have been seeing his ex-wife behind her back. When the ex-wife became pregnant, Libby broke up with Mike and was comforted by a very understanding Drew. Hannah returned, and she and Paul eventually got back together.

Toadfish was falsely accused of culpable driving when his car was stolen and crashed, badly injuring a passenger. A witness was found and he was cleared. Joel resumed studying marine biology and fell for Libby's enemy, Geri. Geri was no fool, though, and worked out Drew was a great catch. She tried to persuade Drew that Libby and he could never amount to anything, since they hadn't even kissed. This backfired when Drew decided she was right, and so he finally kissed Libby.

Sarah moved on, this time to a doctor who wasn't married. Peter, her fiance, put up with her pre-wedding jitters until the wedding day came and she was stranded without transport. Karl offered her a lift. But "The Thunderbird", surely one of the least reliable cars in television history , broke down on the way to the church. The pair arrived, together again for all to see, in a police car.

Sarah was married, much to Susan's relief, and was about to leave for Amsterdam. Nevertheless, Karl's emotional goodbye ended in one last kiss. Susan, less than pleased with Karl turning up with Sarah again, reconnected with an old boyfriend, Michael. When he confessed his love for her, she found it hard to resist. She did, and when Karl went missing, the couple's new resolve led them to counselling.

The Martins left, leaving Lance and Anne behind. Harold collapsed while on lollypop-man duties, and was found to have been poisoned by a weedkiller Lou had been using on his property. The Scullys arrived, with three girls who got the locals talking. Steph liked Drew, but then found out about Libby. Flick had eyes for Billy, who still cared for Anne, while Michelle came to grips with Paul having a crush on Flick. Tess Bell also arrived, to teach at Erinsborough High. Toadfish was about to move out with his girlfriend Charlie, but discovered she was only interested in him to help her secure a residency visa. Joel posed for a nude calendar and worked as a stripper, briefly dating single mum, Natalie.

A millennium party attracted the lovebirds. Anne and Bill shared a kiss again and Drew proposed to Libby. A private moment turned very public when the music stopped just as he was shouting the final line of his proposal. Right then, 26 Ramsay Street burst into flames, and Lolly and Michelle were rescued from inside. As ambulances screamed away, the credits rolled.

1999

Drew and Susan and Karl were thrilled that Libby had said yes to Drew's proposal, only to find that she had actually said no, that she wasn't ready. Lolly and Michelle were treated successfully in hospital after the fire. Tess, the new girl in town, revealed to Susan that her husband was abusing her. Susan organised for her to move out with Anne, but her husband continued to hassle her.

Amy cheated on Lance and became pregnant. She decided to keep the baby, but had a hard time persuading anyone Lance was the father, since they'd never slept together. Bill got an exciting job in Queensland and had to leave almost as soon as he found out, much to Anne's dismay. Tad was hospitalised after excessive drinking, so he decided to pull himself together and trace his real parents. Toadfish used his time-honoured method of winning beautiful women by pretending to be someone else when he and Joel met Dione and Vanessa; the boys pretended to be rich. Joel fell for Dione. Toadie was sad when old friend Bill left town. Anne soon got a transfer and left to be with him, surprising him at the station. Amy married the father of her child and she and Lance made up just before she left.

Flick and Joe had a huge row about Flick's new boyfriend and Flick ran away. Joe persuaded her to return. Tad started working as a DJ at a nightclub, Hemisfear. He found his real mother, Rachel Bailey, but was saddened to learn his father had died. Later, Rachel also died and his half-brother was sick, in desperate need of a bone marrow transplant. Tad saved his life by becoming a donor, and everyone noted how far he'd come. Steph was popular when Lance and Toadfish pursued her in what seemed a fight to the death. She wasn't interested and they eventually backed off. Harold bought a café called Grease Monkeys. Libby accepted Drew's second proposal but then Tess' ex-husband, furious after seeing her with Daniel, caused a terrible accident, hitting

Libby and Steph's motorbike and leaving Libby fighting for her life. Daniel died in hospital, and Libby recovered to be told by doctors that it was unlikely she would be able to have children. She broke up with Drew to spare him the pain, which only caused him more pain.

Michelle stood up to bullies at her school and found an ally in Bianca. Joel and Dee's tempestuous relationship finally came to end. Karl incorrectly cleared a woman of cancer and came up against legal action, which he managed to defeat. Harold was in trouble when he saw a police photograph of a wanted criminal from Tasmania who looked exactly like him. Not being able to remember that part of his life, he suspected he might have been involved and turned himself in. He was selected out of a line-up but saved at the last moment when a witness described a tattoo on the criminal that Harold didn't have.

Drew went on a camping trip with Steph, who confessed her feelings to him. He was tempted, but wasn't over Libby and so he decided he had to leave town. Libby stopped him at the last minute by saying she did love him and would marry him after all. Drew was deliriously happy. Steph was devastated. Dee made friends with Susan's nephew, Doctor Darcy Tyler. Steph was contacted by her ex-boyfriend, Woody, who had been released from prison and wanted to see her.

Less dramatically, Lance was defeated in the student elections by an unknown contender, Sandy Swimmer, who turned out to be Toadfish. Flick had a brief crush on the postman. Michelle won the chance to meet her favorite band, boy4, but they turned out to be obnoxious jerks.

Lance convinced his new girlfriend Lisa that he was adventurous, but had to confess the truth when she took him sky-diving and he couldn't get out of the plane. Joe had to deliver a woman's baby when his cab was trapped in the middle of a fire. Lance finally found the oddball of his dreams when he was asked to complete seven tasks in order to spend the night with a science-fiction addict, Allana Truman. One of these tasks was to shoot his own sci-fi film. He cast Flick and Joel as lovers, and Flick and Joel developed a friendship, much to Joe's fury, and eventually kissed.

2000

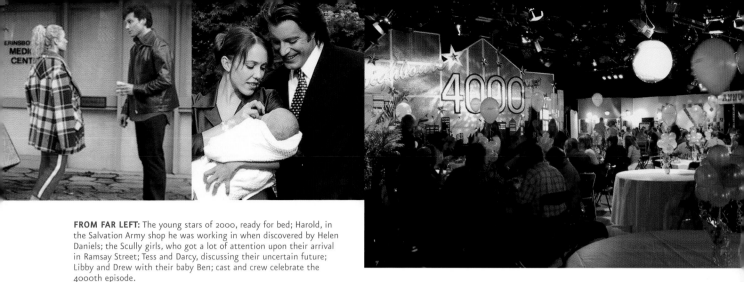

FROM FAR LEFT: The young stars of 2000, ready for bed; Harold, in the Salvation Army shop he was working in when discovered by Helen Daniels; the Scully girls, who got a lot of attention upon their arrival in Ramsay Street; Tess and Darcy, discussing their uncertain future; Libby and Drew with their baby Ben; cast and crew celebrate the 4000th episode.

*I*n the fine *Neighbours* history of disapproving fathers, Joe banned Flick from seeing Joel, causing her to announce she was moving in with him. But sharing a place with Joel and his ex-girlfriend Dee led to tensions, and Joel and Flick eventually broke up. Joe was also worried when Woody made contact with Steph. To Joe's relief, Woody stole some jewellery and was sent back to jail.

Madge was diagnosed with cancer and Harold decided to take her to Paris. Lou even paid for the tickets, but life didn't work out how Harold had hoped it would, and Madge died at home with Harold, Paul and Tad by her side. Her last wish was for Harold to go and see Paris for her, so he and Paul went on the trip and Harold was talked into staying in Erinsborough when he came home. Darcy and Dee got together. Lance and Allana went to America to attend a sci-fi convention.

Drew and Libby's wedding day arrived. The day went well, with a kilted-up Drew singing to Libby, who discovered she was pregnant, a mixed blessing given her health problems. When Dee was sick, Darcy took Tess to the opera and they had an affair. Dee discovered them together and both women dumped Darcy. Karl and Susan were also furious with Darcy for trying to swindle them out of the medical practice.

Woody was released on parole and came to live with the Scullys. He was a marked man, though, and with gangs after him for giving evidence against them in an upcoming trial, he had to go into witness protection. Steph was miserable. She soon found out where Woody lived and the couple had a secret relationship. Woody asked her to leave her family and to come into witness protection with him. She went with him, but when Woody sped away in his car after doing a runner at a petrol station, she couldn't believe her eyes. She chased him, and watched the car explode. Woody was gone.

The Hancocks moved into the old Martin house when Tess and Dee couldn't afford to buy it. Susan had a fight on her hands when Jess Fielding accused her of hitting her in an argument. Tad, who was dating Jess, uncovered the truth and broke up with her for lying. For reasons only Toadfish could justify, he pretended to date Laura Wallace, who actually had a crush on Matt Hancock. But Matt was furious when he discovered Laura was a stripper. She quit, but got him a job as an Elvis impersonator with the same agency, with Flick playing Priscilla Presley.

Darcy proposed to Tess. They were about to marry when Tess decided it was a bad idea, so she apologised to Dee, and left to live with her mother. Dee then discovered she was pregnant with Darcy's baby. She had a miscarriage and only Toadfish knew. Later, she started dating Joel. Lou was so affronted when a man claimed he was Lolly's father that he had a DNA test. But Lou wasn't Lolly's dad. After a long battle, the courts granted the "real" parents custody. That didn't stop Lou kidnapping Lolly, but eventually he faced the music. Lolly was gone. Paul was selected for the Adelaide Crows football team and left Erinsborough.

Tad collapsed after too much alcohol and a scorpion bite on school camp, then confessed his love for Flick, who decided to spend the night with him, but they decided they were better as friends. Steph was seeing Mitch, but getting mysterious deposits into her bank account, which turned out to be from Woody, who had faked his own death as part of the witness protection program. He proposed. Libby gave birth in a barn at a rodeo but while recovering, she had a heart attack…

2001

Libby emerged from her coma, much to Drew's delight. This made Steph miserable, since she wasn't interested in Mitch or Woody, but Drew. Dee broke up with Joel after he revealed Dee's miscarriage to Darcy. Joel eventually left. Evan ran against Joe in the council elections. He found an unlikely ally in Michelle, who launched a spirited campaign against her father and Evan was elected.

Stuart arrived and got together with Dee for a short time. Toadfish and Maggie got work together, and Toadfish developed a crush on Maggie that progressed to a kiss. Tad toured America. Libby decided her new neighbour Terri was a prostitute, but it turned she was an undercover policewoman. Steph met Marc, and Flick also met a man. She asked him out, but he had a girlfriend. She gave him her phone number in case things didn't work out with the girlfriend, but was horrified to find the girlfriend was Steph. Soon, Marc proposed to Steph. When Flick was fired, Marc was her shoulder to cry on, until suddenly they were kissing.

Malcom Kennedy returned to try and wrestle the Coffee Shop from Harold so the company he worked for, Cuppa Diem, could own it. The takeover got nasty and Mal left. Connor arrived at the Scully house and started seeing Michelle. Matt started drag racing and drove off the road into Harold, who was temporarily blinded. The driver of another car was left fighting for his life. Matt fled to avoid manslaughter charges. Maggie and Evan couldn't afford a QC, so they sold their house. Emily proved to be Maggie's undoing, however, when she read the mail aloud from the kitchen table, including a letter from Toadie declaring his love. The family decided to make a new start and left.

Flick saved Lou and Rosie from the burning church and confessed her love to Marc, but decided to resign herself to the marriage. Then Marc turned to her during his wedding vows and stopped. The marriage was off.

A huge fight ensued, with Flick being pursued by Stuart and Marc. Her father and sister wouldn't talk to her, so she moved out. Stuart always defended her and when he left for the army, Flick set out to tell him something but missed him. She broke it off with Marc, and was pleased when Stuart returned. Summer and Boyd Hoyland arrived, followed by Max. Tad went to the Extreme Games in America. He was joined by Flick, desperate to escape.

Susan fell over and was diagnosed with amnesia. She soon remembered Karl's affair and demanded a divorce. Summer was diagnosed with Long QT Syndrome, which her mother died of. Connor admitted he was illiterate after putting floor cleaner in Michelle's drink. Flick returned. Joe talked Lyn into having another baby, but Michelle was unsupportive. When Flick told her how little sisters look up to their big sisters, though, Michelle softened. Steph, eavesdropping, also softened, and started to forgive Flick.

Drew, on his first day of a new life on Ron's farm with Libby, fell off his horse and died. Flick and Stuart decided to get together after discussing it with Steph. Nina recorded her own song, *Born to Try*, and Connor entered it in a talent contest, which she won but was too nervous to receive. Tahnee received it in her place, but Connor put a stop to it. Tahnee then told Michelle about Nina's feelings for Connor, and the couple broke up. Nina convinced them she posed no threat. Steph told Max she disapproved of his parenting skills, but Libby suspected they liked each other. Boyd told Max that Steph wasn't interested.

Lou collapsed and was diagnosed with serious kidney problems. Flick, about to leave for New York, was thrilled when Stuart proposed to her. Dee and Toadfish kissed in a game of dare and Dee decided Toadie was the one for her. Darcy confessed his love for Chloe while tied up by burglars, but Chloe broke up with him when he flirted with Dee. Nina and Taj started dating. Karl and Susan decided to marry at Lassiters. At the wedding, Susan recited her original wedding vows, and her memory returned. Joe caught Michelle and Connor at the wedding and demanded they explain a positive pregnancy test he found. Lyn stepped in and explained she was pregnant.

2002

FROM FAR LEFT: Steph throws a punch at her sister in the dramatic aftermath of her wedding; Drew and Libby together on the farm; Stuart, who was involved in a cult; Lou and Trixie become man and wife; Nina Tucker, the shy girl with the beautiful voice, finally has the confidence to sing.

Nina and Jack played lovers rather convincingly in Harold's community play, which led to an affair. Ruby, Harold's lady friend from the dating agency, admitted she had a gambling problem and had robbed No.24. Darcy used every dirty trick in the book to split Dee and Toadfish up. Then he moved in on Dee. Darcy was also gambling excessively. Stuart broke up his engagement to Flick to be with Libby, who rejected him. Karl was charged for drink driving and was represented in court by Toadfish. They lost and Karl's drinking got worse.

Connor took Joe's place at work temporarily and was reported to immigration for being in Australia illegally. After almost marrying Michelle and skipping the country, he stayed. Nina broke up with Taj to be with Jack, but Lori was badly hurt in a poolside accident so Jack felt he couldn't break up with her. Lori and Taj found out about the affair. Nina didn't want to hurt anyone so she and Jack remained single.

After trying to make it with Max, Steph started going out with new barman Alex. They went on holiday but broke up and Steph came home to Max, whose kids took a while to warm to them being a couple. Tahnee was sent home from exchange and replaced by Michelle. Tahnee's parents sent her to boarding school. Valda returned. After much prodding, she eventually told Lou her secret: she was Lyn's mother. Darcy gambled away $60,000 and robbed the pub and then the Kennedys, where he knocked Lyn unconscious. Ruby was arrested but Lyn's memory returned and Dee, heartbroken, backed up Lyn's evidence that it was Darcy. Darcy was jailed for 18 months. Dee reconciled with Toadfish, and they got engaged. Lyn discovered Valda's secret and eventually forgave her parents.

Toadfish and Dee married, but the wedding ended in grief when Toadfish was distracted by a kiss and drove the car off a cliff. Dee's body was never found. Devastated, Libby found solace with Taj for a night. Nina and Jack got together causing a bereft Lori and Connor to sleep together. Lori fell pregnant and left for New Zealand. Jack slept with Edwina not long before sleeping with Nina for the first time.

Stuart was a suspect in Dee's death because the car's brakes were faulty. Toadfish was furious but was shocked when the coroner instead found him guilty of culpable driving. Their friendship suffered. Taj told Nina about Jack's cheating. Nina broke it off and turned to Connor. Harold had new houseguests. His granddaughter Sky Mangel returned and his son David and Liljana and Serena moved in. He disapproved of nearly all of them. Steph discovered she had breast cancer and kept it secret to protect Max. Max's sister Izzy arrived and tried to turn his family against Steph. She also started flirting with Karl. After Lyn's baby Oscar was born, Lyn was diagnosed with severe post-natal depression.

Stuart was addicted to a cult called "Life Mechanics", but Taj soon realised it was a con. Stuart sunk deeper and isolated everyone. Steph's cancer was revealed and Max supported her. When the cancer went into remission, Max proposed but Steph said no. Karl and Susan discovered a letter from Daphne Clarke to her son Jamie saying he had a share in a wealthy business. Stuart found Jamie, homeless.

Izzy and Jack had a brief affair but Sky wrongly accused Izzy of having an affair with Karl. Trixie, Nina's mother arrived, straight into the arms of Lou. Nina discovered she was illegitimate and left for India. Connor kissed Carmella, the daughter of a mafia boss. Serena met dodgy Chris Cousens, who invited her to model for him for cash if she spent the night with him. Karl was found secretly drinking with Izzy so Susan left for Adelaide for Christmas. Lou and Trixie got married and Harold collapsed at the wedding, alone and in the dark.

2003

2004

7his year had everything: a reality TV show, a girl-on-girl kiss, an exploding Lassiters, and even a nasty, boozy, meat-eating Harold. Harold recovered from his stroke, but it affected his personality. He was rude, obnoxious, boozy, and he rejected both his vegetarianism and his Christianity. He soon recovered.

Sky, contrary to Harold's advice, met the man who accidentally killed her mother. She came to terms with her loss after a major image change. Trixie convinced Lou to put all his money into a production of *Hello Dolly*, but Lou lost all his money ... and Trixie.

Mafia man Rocco found out about Carmella and Connor, so Carmella was sent to Italy. When Michelle returned, Connor broke it off with Carmella, only to find his ex-partner Lori was in town with Maddy, their baby. Michelle, torn between her career in New York and Connor, chose New York.

Liljana's meddling mother, Svetlanka, arrived, revealing that Lil was pregnant when she met David. Lil confessed she had had a child who she never met. The Scully family's appalling application for reality TV show, *Making Mansions*, was successful. But although the house was transformed, the family was portrayed as a bunch of hicks.

Max's "friend" Gus turned up to romance Izzy. Mal returned and fought with Karl, who moved out. Joe left for Bendigo. Toadie developed a typically hair-brained scheme to get Taj noticed by a producer.

In the end Taj got a job as a runner on a film in Sydney. Gus spied on Izzy and discovered she was pregnant. He knew it was his baby but Izzy had him taken away to a psychiatric hospital and moved into Karl's flat, pretending he was the father.

Darcy, on day release, discovered the truth but when he fell down the stairs at the hospital, Izzy made it look like he had robbed her. Karl proposed to Izzy on a boat, but she fell in. At the hospital, she had a flashback of Darcy falling down the stairs, and down she toppled. The baby didn't survive. Gus turned up at their wedding, causing Izzy to flee. Karl later forgave her.

Susan found love with Joe Scully's brother, who was Lyn's old flame and a Catholic priest. Lyn disapproved and Tom was torn. He chose Susan, but the strain was too much so he left. Libby called an electrician who turned out to be Darren.

Jack started taking drugs with a girl called Mac. Stuart joined the police force and was partnered with Sgt. Olivia McPherson. Mac and Olivia turned out to be the same person, and her corruption was revealed as she and Jack pinned their crimes on Darren. Jack crashed his car and Stuart turned Olivia, now his girlfriend, in to police.

Not even Libby believed Darren was innocent, causing him to leave town. Even after Libby won a hot date with her favourite soapie star, she still missed Darren, so she left to be with him. Steph and Max eloped to the country to have a relaxed ceremony.

Toadie's mischievous cousin Stingray arrived. When Toadie went missing, Stuart knew Rocco had sought revenge after Toadie stole Sindi from him. Sure enough, Toadie was in a coma and Rocco was charged.

Lou, in jail due to his racing scam with Rocco, was released after an appeal. Nina returned to ask Jack to come to America. Susan and Karl divorced, sharing a kiss goodbye.

Lana kissed Sky but ran off crying. They kissed again, but Sky wasn't interested, hurting Lana. Then Boyd broke up with Sky.

Luka arrived. He and Serena were about to sleep together when Liljana collapsed. The truth emerged: Luka was the child Lil never got to see. Luka left afterwards. Carmella reunited with Connor.

Sindi and Stuart found love in a bank siege. Lyn divorced Joe. Steph was blamed for her grandfather's death. Then, someone set Lassiters on fire with Stuart and Sindi inside. Paul Robinson – back at last – watched the burning building. ●

1

4

2

3

5

7 8

6

9

10

As *Neighbours* celebrated its 20th year, the drama and intrigue continued apace. Here's a pictorial celebration of the year's highlights so far ...

1. Sky is interrogated by police following the murder of Gus Cleary. 2. Sindi returns to her past career of exotic dancing, desperately trying to raise money for an operation to restore Stuart's sight. 3. Creepy Chris Cousens endangers Janae's safety in a night spot, before Janae escapes his clutches with the help of her siblings, Stingray and Bree. 4. Stuart takes off his bandages for the first time after losing his sight trying to save Sindi in the 2004 fire finale. He was almost completely blind. 5. Connor faces death when Carmella's stalker ties him up in an abandoned building – luckily he escapes before it is demolished. 6. Sky comforts Boyd in hospital. He was wrongly diagnosed with schizophrenia – actually he had a brain tumour. Serena (standing behind Sky) guiltily hid the fact that she had pashed Boyd when he and Sky had broken up. It was later revealed and Sky and Boyd broke up. 7. Sky confronts Serena about pashing Boyd – a big betrayal from her cousin who is like a sister to her. 8. Liljana succumbs to passion with evil Paul Robinson, despite her marriage to David Bishop. 9. Harold stands outside his new General Store, which is opened with Lou Carpenter, after his Coffee Shop burnt down in the Lassiter's fire in the 2004 season finale. 10. The 2005 cast and crew.

2005

Character List

The main players over the first 20 years of Ramsay Street.

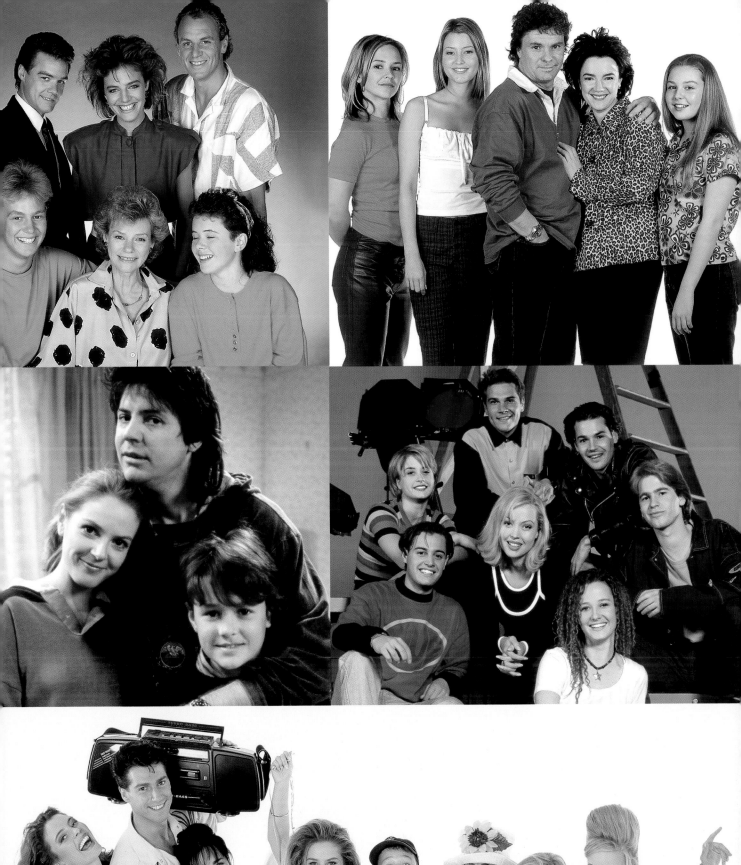

Benito **Alessi**

FIRST APPEARED 1992

LAST APPEARED 1993 > Went to Sydney to take up a top executive job.

PLAYED BY George Spartels

Caroline **Alessi**

FIRST APPEARED 1990

LAST APPEARED 1992 > Went to Milan to follow dream of managing a hotel.

PLAYED BY Gillian Blakeney

INTERESTING FACT The closest Caroline got to having a child on the show was when she had sympathetic labor pains while Christina was having Andrew.

Catherine **Alessi**

FIRST APPEARED 1992

LAST APPEARED 1993 > Went to Sydney with husband Benito.

PLAYED BY Elspeth Ballantyne

INTERESTING FACT When Catherine and Benito left for Sydney, it was the first overt reference to Melbourne being the home of Ramsay Street.

Christina **Alessi Robinson**

FIRST APPEARED 1990

LAST APPEARED 1992 > Went to Hawaii to run a hotel.

PLAYED BY Gayle Blakeney

INTERESTING FACT Gayle and sister Chrissie first came to town as one person, "Linda Giles", due to the peculiar requirements of a witness protection program. Their secret was uncovered when Paul realised "Linda" fluctuated wildly between being exceptional and dreadful at work.

Marco **Alessi**

FIRST APPEARED 1992

LAST APPEARED 1992 > Ran away to Italy to avoid loan sharks – lives with his family.

PLAYED BY Felice Arena

INTERESTING FACT Felice Arena wrote the extremely successful children's book, *Specky Magee*, with Australian Rules footballer Garry Lyon.

Rick **Alessi**

FIRST APPEARED 1992

LAST APPEARED 1995 > Left to be assistant food and beverages manager at Lassiters in Darwin.

PLAYED BY Dan Falzon

INTERESTING FACT Rick's driving instructor was in fact a dummy he named "Roy". When Roy was about to be discovered by suspicious neighbours, Rick threw him over a cliff, only to watch in dismay as Lou's car went tumbling after him.

Josh **Anderson**

FIRST APPEARED 1990

LAST APPEARED 1991

PLAYED BY Jeremy Angerson

Ben **Atkins**

FIRST APPEARED 1997

LAST APPEARED 1998 > Left to work in a garage with his real father in Sydney.

PLAYED BY Brett Cousins

INTERESTING FACT Anne had a crush on Ben until he revealed to her that he was her half-brother.

Caitlin **Atkins**

FIRST APPEARED 1997

LAST APPEARED 1998 > Left to be with her mother.

PLAYED BY Emily Milburn

INTERESTING FACT When she left, she painted a farewell message on the road.

Nicholas **Atkins**

FIRST APPEARED 1998

LAST APPEARED 1998

PLAYED BY Jason Crewe

INTERESTING FACT Nick spent some time early on pretending to be Toadie for the benefit of Karen, one of Toadie's fans. Toadie didn't think she'd be interested in him once she knew he wasn't the handsome Nick.

Sarah **Beaumont**

FIRST APPEARED 1996.

LAST APPEARED 1999 > Went to start a life with Peter Hannay in Amsterdam. Cameo appearance in 2005.

PLAYED BY Nicola Charles

INTERESTING FACT Sarah was chased across the world by her ex-fiancé, a British Lord.

Theresa (Tess) **Bell**

FIRST APPEARED 1999

LAST APPEARED 2001 > Went to Sydney to join her family and then to UK for work.

PLAYED BY Krista Vendy

INTERESTING FACT In real life, Krista is the cousin of Kristian Schmid (Todd Landers).

David **Bishop**

APPEARED 1998, 2003

LAST APPEARED Still present.

PLAYED BY Kevin Harrington

Harold **Bishop**

APPEARED 1987 - 1991. 1996. 1997

LAST APPEARED Still present.

PLAYED BY Ian Smith

INTERESTING FACT Ian Smith is the longest-serving member of the *Neighbours* cast and also has written for the show.

Kerry **Bishop**

FIRST APPEARED 1989

LAST APPEARED 1990 > Died when shot by a stray bullet at a duck shooting protest.

PLAYED BY Linda Hartley

INTERESTING FACT In 1985, Linda Hartley guest-starred as Gloria Slater. She also starred in *Prisoner*.

Liljana **Bishop**

FIRST APPEARED 2003

LAST APPEARED Still present.

PLAYED BY Marcella Russo

INTERESTING FACT Liljana is the first Serbian resident of Ramsay Street.

Madge **Bishop**

APPEARED 1986 - 1992. 1996. 1997 - 2001.

LAST APPEARED 2001 > died (cancer)

PLAYED BY Anne Charleston

INTERESTING FACT Also starred in *Prisoner* and *The Sullivans*.

Serena **Bishop**

FIRST APPEARED 2003

LAST APPEARED Still present.

PLAYED BY Lara Sacher

INTERESTING FACT Despite the publicity generated by an "incest" plotline, Serena Bishop is not the only character on *Neighbours* to discover she was related to the person she had a crush on. Ben Atkins had to reveal to Anne Wilkinson that he couldn't be with her because she was his half-sister, and Lucy Robinson and Glen were also nearly involved in an incestuous relationship.

Dione (Dee) **Bliss**

FIRST APPEARED 2000

LAST APPEARED 2003 > Presumed dead.

PLAYED BY Madeleine West

INTERESTING FACT Madeleine West is now a stand-up comedian.

Bouncer

FIRST APPEARED 1987

LAST APPEARED 1993 > Went to live with Dorothy Burke and Toby Mangel in the country.

INTERESTING FACT Bouncer, like most of the Ramsay Street residents, had a true love: sheepdog Rosie, who rescued Bouncer from a manhole. Bouncer once had a dream he married Rosie.

Beth **Brennan Willis**

FIRST APPEARED 1991

LAST APPEARED 1993 > Married Brad and left for Perth.

PLAYED BY Natalie Imbruglia

INTERESTING FACT Went on to become a successful singer and actor.
In 2002, Natalie signed a six-figure contract with L'Oreal.

Eddie **Buckingham**

FIRST APPEARED 1990
LAST APPEARED 1990 > Left to care for his sick father.
PLAYED BY Bob La Castra

Dorothy **Bourke**

FIRST APPEARED 1990
LAST APPEARED 1993 > Went to live with Tom in the country.
PLAYED BY Maggie Dence

Carmella **Camminetti**

FIRST APPEARED 2003
LAST APPEARED Still present.
PLAYED BY Natalie Blair

Guy **Carpenter**

FIRST APPEARED 1991
LAST APPEARED 1992 > Left to be a swimming instructor in Broome.
PLAYED BY Andrew Williams

Lauren **Carpenter**

FIRST APPEARED 1993
LAST APPEARED 1994 > Left for Queensland to run a riding school.
PLAYED BY Sarah Vandenbergh
INTERESTING FACT Lauren literally rode into Erinsborough on a horse.

Lou **Carpenter**

APPEARED 1988. 1991.
LAST APPEARED Still present.
PLAYED BY Tom Oliver
INTERESTING FACT Lou was brought back in 1997 due to popular demand.

Louise (Lolly) **Carpenter**

FIRST APPEARED 1994
LAST APPEARED 2001 > Lou lost custody, Lolly went to live with the Allens.
PLAYED BY Tessa Taylor (1994); Jiordan Anna Tolli (1994 - 2001)
INTERESTING FACT When custody of Lolly was being decided, she was at a Wiggles concert. Jiordan is Kym Valentine's cousin by marriage.

Edith **Chubb**

FIRST APPEARED 1988
LAST APPEARED 1989 > Left to help a sick relative.
PLAYED BY Irene Inescort

Daphne **Clarke**

FIRST APPEARED 1985
LAST APPEARED 1988 > Died after a car accident.
PLAYED BY Elaine Smith

Des **Clarke**

FIRST APPEARED 1985
LAST APPEARED 1990 > Married a widow, Fiona, in Perth.
PLAYED BY Paul Keane

Eileen **Clarke**

FIRST APPEARED 1985
LAST APPEARED 1988 > Got married in England.
PLAYED BY Myra De Groot
INTERESTING FACT Eileen never would have made it to England if Malcom hadn't won tickets in a game show. The Ramsay Street residents have an abnormally high percentage of wins in game shows. They've won on date shows, renovation shows, quiz shows, and reality TV shows.

Jamie **Clarke**

FIRST APPEARED 1987 . 2003.
LAST APPEARED 2003 > Stuart Parker found Jamie living on the streets.
PLAYED BY SJ Dey; Ryder Susman; Nicholas Mason; James Mason, Angus McLaren
INTERESTING FACT Jamie Clarke was played by a girl for two years (SJ Dey is Sarah Jane).

Susan **Cole**

FIRST APPEARED 1986
LAST APPEARED 1987 > Left after Clive broke up with her.
PLAYED BY Gloria Ajenstat
INTERESTING FACT Guest-starred in original series as Nurse Stevens.

Elly **Conway**

FIRST APPEARED 2001
LAST APPEARED 2002 > Moved to Sweden with her real mother.
PLAYED BY Kendall Nunn

Taj **Coppin**

FIRST APPEARED 2002
LAST APPEARED 2004 > Became a runner on a film set.
PLAYED BY Jaime Robbie Reyne

Helen **Daniels**

FIRST APPEARED 1985

LAST APPEARED 1997 > Died.

PLAYED BY Anne Haddy

Rosemary **Daniels**

FIRST APPEARED 1985

LAST APPEARED 1998 > Returned to New York to run her companies.

PLAYED BY Joy Chambers

INTERESTING FACT Joy Chambers is a successful novelist and businesswoman. She is also married to Reg Grundy, the founder of the Grundy organisation.

Bronwyn **Davies**

FIRST APPEARED 1988

LAST APPEARED 1990 > Went to live in New Zealand with Henry.

PLAYED BY Rachel Friend

INTERESTING FACT Three years after her time playing the love of Henry's life on *Neighbours*, Rachel Friend wed the real life Henry, Craig McLachlan. They were married for a year.

Sharon **Davies**

FIRST APPEARED 1988

LAST APPEARED 1990 > Went to New Zealand to live with Bronwyn.

PLAYED BY Jessica Muschamp

Zoe **Davis**

FIRST APPEARED 1986

LAST APPEARED 1986 > Left to marry another man after turning down Jim's proposal.

PLAYED BY Ally Fowler

INTERESTING FACT Alexandra (Ally) Fowler was the lead singer of The Chantoozies with David Reyne and Tottie Goldsmith. She also played the lead role in *Sons & Daughters*.

Laura **Dennison**

FIRST APPEARED 1986

LAST APPEARED 1986 > Left for America for multiple sclerosis treatment.

PLAYED BY Carole Skinner

INTERESTING FACT Starred in both *Prisoner* and *Moulin Rouge*.

Nikki **Dennison**

FIRST APPEARED 1986

LAST APPEARED 1986 > Left for America to be with her mother.

PLAYED BY Charlene Fenn

Glen **Donnelly**

FIRST APPEARED 1990

LAST APPEARED 1992 > Disappeared with Karen and Rose. Nobody knows his whereabouts.

PLAYED BY Richard Huggett

INTERESTING FACT Biggest talking point after Glen's arrival was the plot line where Glen kissed his half-sister, Lucy.

Wayne **Duncan**

FIRST APPEARED 1993

LAST APPEARED 1994 > Left teaching at Erinsborough High to go back to the farm.

PLAYED BY Jonathon Sammy-Lee

Lisa **Elliot**

FIRST APPEARED 1997

LAST APPEARED 1997

PLAYED BY Kate Straub

INTERESTING FACT Kate Straub was given the role on *Neighbours* after being spotted in the audience of TV show *Hey Hey It's Saturday*.

Clive **Gibbons**

APPEARED 1986 - 1987. 1989.

LAST APPEARED 1989 > Left to run a surgery in the country.

PLAYED BY Geoff Paine

Hope **Gottlieb**

FIRST APPEARED 1993

LAST APPEARED 1993 > Left with her family to Anson's Corner.

PLAYED BY Laura Pearson

Mark **Gottlieb**

FIRST APPEARED 1993

LAST APPEARED 1995

PLAYED BY Bruce Samazan

INTERESTING FACT Mark was originally named "Cosmic" by his hippie parents.

Phoebe **Gottlieb**

FIRST APPEARED 1991

LAST APPEARED 1993 > Left to run a record shop at Anson's Corner with Stephen.

PLAYED BY Simone Robertson

INTERESTING FACT Simone Robertson was for a time romantically linked to Benjamin Mitchell (Cameron Hudson).

Serendipity (Ren) **Gottlieb**

FIRST APPEARED 1994

LAST APPEARED 1995 > Left with Luke who a got job teaching English in Japan.

PLAYED BY Raelee Hill

INTERESTING FACT Her nickname, spread around Ramsay Street by her brothers before she arrived, was "Dippy the Hippie" due to her alternative lifestyle.

Stephen **Gottlieb**

FIRST APPEARED 1992

LAST APPEARED 1993 > Left with Phoebe to Anson's corner to open a record shop.

PLAYED BY Lochie Daddo

INTERESTING FACT Stephen was originally Christened "Freedom" by his parents.

Amy **Greenwood**

FIRST APPEARED 1997.

LAST APPEARED 2000 > Left to get married to Damien. Cameo appearance in 2005.

PLAYED BY Jacinta Stapleton

INTERESTING FACT Jacinta Stapleton's brother, Sullivan Stapleton, played the role of Josh Hughes.

Emily **Hancock**

FIRST APPEARED 2001

LAST APPEARED 2001 > Left to live at her grandparents' house with family.

PLAYED BY Isabella Oldham

INTERESTING FACT Emily's best friend was the ghost of Madge.

Evan **Hancock**

FIRST APPEARED 2001

LAST APPEARED 2002 > Left to sort out his marriage problems with Maggie.

PLAYED BY Nicholas Opolski

Leo **Hancock**

FIRST APPEARED 2001

LAST APPEARED 2002 > Left with his family.

PLAYED BY Josh Jay; Anthony Hammer

INTERESTING FACT Leo harboured an illegal immigrant from the fictional Baruhstan with whom he shared an obsessive interest in Kung Fu TV shows.

Matt **Hancock**

FIRST APPEARED 2001.

LAST APPEARED 2002 > Moved to Albury with family. Cameo appearance in 2005.

PLAYED BY Stephen Hunt

INTERESTING FACT Matt's jobs included working in the bar, working with Steph, working as an Elvis impersonator and illegal drag racing.

Jen **Handley**

FIRST APPEARED 1995

LAST APPEARED 1996 > Was awarded an art scholarship in the Northern Territory.

PLAYED BY Alyce Platt

INTERESTING FACT Jen was addicted to a soap opera called *Stairwells of Time*.

Luke **Handley**

FIRST APPEARED 1995.

LAST APPEARED 1996 > Left when Danni caught malaria in Malaysia. They settled there. Cameo appearance in 2005.

PLAYED BY Bernard Curry

INTERESTING FACT Bernard Curry is the brother of two other *Neighbours* stars: Andrew (who played Larry Woodhouse) and Stephen (Greg Bartlett).

Jane **Harris**

FIRST APPEARED 1986.

LAST APPEARED 1989 > Moved to England with Mrs Mangel, calling off her wedding to Des at the last minute. Cameo appearance in 2005.

PLAYED BY Annie Jones

INTERESTING FACT Annie Jones was born Annika Jansco.

Annalise **Hartman**

FIRST APPEARED 1993.

LAST APPEARED 1996 > Followed her business to the UK. Settled there with Sam. Cameo appearance in 2005.

PLAYED BY Kimberley Davies

INTERESTING FACT Kimberley Davies has gone on to guest-star in *Friends*, *Spin City* and *Ally McBeal*.

Joanna **Hartman**

APPEARED 1995. 1996 - 1997.

LAST APPEARED 1997 > Returned to Europe to reunite with husband Rob.

PLAYED BY Emma Harrison

INTERESTING FACT Emma Harrison went on to star in *Legally Blonde* and *Intolerable Cruelty*.

Mike **Healey**

FIRST APPEARED 1998

LAST APPEARED 1999 > Left Libby to get on with her life after cheating on her.

PLAYED BY Andrew Blackman

Boyd **Hoyland**

FIRST APPEARED 2002
LAST APPEARED Still present.
PLAYED BY Kyal Marsh

Isabelle **Hoyland**

FIRST APPEARED 2003
LAST APPEARED Still present.
PLAYED BY Natalie Bassingthwaighte
INTERESTING FACT Before her time on Ramsay Street, Izzy ran a llama farm and worked as meter maid.

Max **Hoyland**

FIRST APPEARED 2002
LAST APPEARED Still present.
PLAYED BY Stephen Lovatt

Rosie **Hoyland**

FIRST APPEARED 2002
LAST APPEARED 2003 > Moved to provide help in Papua New Guinea after a cyclone hit there.
PLAYED BY Maggie Millar
INTERESTING FACT When it became clear the character of Rosie was going to leave Ramsay Street, fans launched a campaign (The Rescue Rosie campaign) to prevent her leaving.

Stephanie **Hoyland**

FIRST APPEARED 1999
LAST APPEARED Still present.
PLAYED BY Carla Bonner

Summer **Hoyland**

FIRST APPEARED 2002
LAST APPEARED Still present.
PLAYED BY Marisa Siketa

Cameron **Hudson**

FIRST APPEARED 1992
LAST APPEARED 1993 > Left when heartbroken by Lauren Carpenter and Brad Willis' romance.
PLAYED BY Benjamin Mitchell
INTERESTING FACT The role of his rival, Brad Willis, was originally played by Benjamin Mitchell himself for one episode.

Faye **Hudson**

FIRST APPEARED 1991
LAST APPEARED 1992 > Ran away in the middle of the night after accidentally burning Lassiter's fashion boutique to the ground and being sued for the damages. Last heard of in Paris.
PLAYED BY Lorraine Bayly

Melissa **Jarrett**

FIRST APPEARED 1989

LAST APPEARED 1991 > Went to live in America when her father landed a job there.

PLAYED BY Jade Amenta

INTERESTING FACT When Melissa left Erinsborough, she was presented with a year's supply of Vegemite to remind her of home.

Billy **Kennedy**

FIRST APPEARED 1994.

LAST APPEARED 2000 > Landed an apprenticeship in Queensland with a woodworker. Later joined by Anne. Cameo appearance in 2005.

PLAYED BY Jesse Spencer

INTERESTING FACT The episode where Billy lost his virginity was originally not screened in the United Kingdom. It later was.

Karl **Kennedy**

FIRST APPEARED 1994

LAST APPEARED Still present.

PLAYED BY Alan Fletcher

INTERESTING FACT Karl Kennedy was named after Karl Marx, by his socialist father. Alan Fletcher plays Jackie Woodburne's husband in *Neighbours*, but played opposite her once before in *Cop Shop*, as her brother.

Libby **Kennedy**

FIRST APPEARED 1994.

LAST APPEARED 2004 > Left to be with Darren in Shepparton. Cameo appearance in 2005.

PLAYED BY Kym Valentine

INTERESTING FACT Kym Valentine's cousin by marriage is Jiordan Anna Tolli, who played the role of Louise Carpenter. Kym recently appeared in the stage production of *Dirty Dancing* in Australia.

Malcolm **Kennedy**

FIRST APPEARED 1994 -1997. 2002. 2004.

LAST APPEARED 2004 > Moved to London to restart work there at Cuppa Diem. Cameo appearance in 2005.

PLAYED BY Benjamin McNair (also Benjie, Benjii and Benji)

Ben **Kirk**

FIRST APPEARED 2001

LAST APPEARED 2004 > Left with Libby and Darren to live in Shepparton.

PLAYED BY Noah Sutherland; Sean Berends

INTERESTING FACT Ben's middle name is Ian, a tribute to the late Ian Coughlan, who wrote for the show.

Drew **Kirk**

FIRST APPEARED 1998

LAST APPEARED 2002 > Died when he fell off his horse while riding with Libby.

PLAYED BY Dan Paris

Marlene **Kratz**

FIRST APPEARED 1994.

LAST APPEARED 1997 > Left to go on a cruise. Cameo appearance in 2005.

PLAYED BY Moya O'Sullivan

INTERESTING FACT Marlene left to go on a cruise. She still isn't back because she married the captain.

Sam **Kratz**

FIRST APPEARED 1994

LAST APPEARED 1996 > Left to live in London with Annalise. Cameo appearance in 2005.

PLAYED BY Richard Grieve

Katie **Landers**

FIRST APPEARED 1987

LAST APPEARED 1989 > Returned to Adelaide with her mother.

PLAYED BY Sally Jensen

Todd **Landers**

FIRST APPEARED 1987

LAST APPEARED 1992 > Died when running across the road to tell Phoebe to keep the baby.

PLAYED BY Kristian Schmid

INTERESTING FACT Kristian Schmid is the descendant of a 17th century Austrian Empress' royal courtier. He's also related to Krista Vendy, who played Tessa years later.

Lori **Lee**

APPEARED 2002 - 2003. 2004.

LAST APPEARED 2004 > Left to be PR manager and receptionist in Lorne.

PLAYED BY Michelle Ang

Lee **Maloney**

FIRST APPEARED 1989

LAST APPEARED 1990 > Left Matt broken-hearted and was never found.

PLAYED BY Maree Ackhurst

Joe **Mangel**

FIRST APPEARED 1988

LAST APPEARED Settled in the country in 1991. Returned to visit in 2005.

PLAYED BY Mark Little

Mrs Nell **Mangel**

FIRST APPEARED 1986

LAST APPEARED 1988 > Settled in England with John Worthington.

PLAYED BY Vivean Gray

INTERESTING FACT It is said a central reason for Vivean Gray leaving the show was the abuse she received from the general public on Mrs. Mangel's behalf.

Sky **Mangel**

FIRST APPEARED 1988-1991. 2003.

LAST APPEARED Still present.

PLAYED BY Miranda Fryer; Stephanie McIntosh

INTERESTING FACT Stephanie McIntosh is the half-sister of Jason Donovan, known to *Neighbours* fans as Scott Robinson.

Toby **Mangel**

FIRST APPEARED 1988

LAST APPEARED 1993 > Left with Bouncer to live with Dorothy and Joe.

PLAYED BY Finn Greentree-Keane; Ben Geurens

Debbie **Martin**

APPEARED 1985. 1992-1994. 1996 - 1997.

LAST APPEARED 1997 > Left to be with Michael. Cameo appearance in 2005.

PLAYED BY Mandy Storvik; Marnie Reece-Wilmore

Hannah **Martin**

FIRST APPEARED 1992, Cameo appearance in 2005.

LAST APPEARED 1999 > Left with Philip and Ruth to live in Darwin.

PLAYED BY Rebecca Ritters

Julie **Martin**

FIRST APPEARED 1985. 1992 - 1994.
LAST APPEARED 1994 > Died after falling from a tower at a murder mystery weekend.
PLAYED BY Vikki Blanche; Julie Mullins

Michael **Martin**

FIRST APPEARED 1992
LAST APPEARED 1998 > Moved away to a farm.
PLAYED BY Troy Beckwith
INTERESTING FACT Also played a love interest of Cody.

Philip **Martin**

APPEARED 1985. 1992 - 1999
LAST APPEARED 1999 > Got a new job in Darwin. Cameo appearance in 2005.
PLAYED BY Christopher Milne; Ian Rawlings
INTERESTING FACT Christopher Milne has also written several episodes over the years.

Paul **McClain**

FIRST APPEARED 1997
LAST APPEARED 2001 > Selected to play Australian Rules football for the Adelaide Crows. Cameo appearance in 2005.
PLAYED BY Jansen Spencer
INTERESTING FACT Paul and Harold had a band together in which Paul played electric guitar and Harold played tuba. The band was called Tuba Electrica. They were its only two fans.

Tiffany (Lochy) **McLachlan**

FIRST APPEARED 1989
LAST APPEARED 1990
PLAYED BY Amber Kilpatrick

Ryan **McLachlan**

FIRST APPEARED 1990
LAST APPEARED 1991 > Joined the army.
PLAYED BY Richard Norton

Catherine **O'Brien**

FIRST APPEARED 1996
LAST APPEARED 1997 > Followed Mal to the airport, then to England where they married.
PLAYED BY Radha Mitchell
INTERESTING FACT Radha Mitchell went on to star in Hollywood movies such as *Phone Booth* and *Finding Neverland*. She had earlier starred as a parachute instructor on *Neighbours* before her role as Catherine.

Connor **O'Neill**

FIRST APPEARED 2002

LAST APPEARED Still present.

PLAYED BY Patrick Harvey

INTERESTING FACT When Patrick Harvey auditioned, he did so with an Australian accent. When he re-read the part in his own, Irish accent, he got the role.

Nick **Page**

FIRST APPEARED 1988

LAST APPEARED 1990 > Won an art scholarship in London.

PLAYED BY Mark Stevens

INTERESTING FACT Mark Stevens first appeared on TV in Australia on the talent quest *Young Talent Time*, which produced other Aussie stars such as Dannii Minogue and Tina Arena.

Stuart **Parker**

FIRST APPEARED 2002

LAST APPEARED Still present.

PLAYED BY Blair McDonough

INTERESTING FACT Blair McDonough won the role of Stuart after declaring on reality TV series *Big Brother* that *Neighbours* was his favorite show. He was runner-up on the first series of *Big Brother* and began his role on *Neighbours* not long after the final episode of Big Brother. Later in *Neighbours*, Stuart Parker expressed his disgust at reality television.

Melanie **Pearson**

APPEARED 1987. 1988. 1989 - 1991.

LAST APPEARED 1991 > Settled in the country with Joe, but later left to see the world. Cameo appearance in 2005.

PLAYED BY Lucinda Cowden

Danny **Ramsay**

FIRST APPEARED 1985

LAST APPEARED 1986 > Joined his family in Brisbane after getting a transfer. Cameo appearance in 2005.

PLAYED BY David Clencie

Gemma **Ramsay**

FIRST APPEARED 1990

LAST APPEARED 1991 > Moved to Newcastle and was later joined by Adam Willis.

PLAYED BY Beth Buchanan

INTERESTING FACT Beth Buchanan is the sister of Simone Buchanan, who played Debbie Kelly in the Australian sitcom *Hey Dad!*

Henry **Ramsay**

FIRST APPEARED 1986

LAST APPEARED 1989 > Became a radio announcer in New Zealand. Later joined by Bronwyn.

PLAYED BY Craig McLachlan

INTERESTING FACT Craig McLachlan was married for a short time to his onscreen love interest Rachel Friend (Bronwyn). He co-starred alongside another ex-*Neighbours* star, Delta Goodrem, in the Australian feature film *Hating Alison Ashley*.

Maria **Ramsay**

FIRST APPEARED 1985

LAST APPEARED 1985 > Ran away with the insurance man, Richard Morrison, to Hong Kong. Later, reconciled with Max and lived in Queensland.

PLAYED BY Dasha Blahova

Max **Ramsay**

FIRST APPEARED 1985

LAST APPEARED 1986 > Left to live with Maria again in Brisbane, Queensland.

PLAYED BY Francis Bell

Shane **Ramsay**

FIRST APPEARED 1985

LAST APPEARED 1986 > Travelled around Australia on his motorbike before settling in Queensland.

PLAYED BY Peter O'Brien

INTERESTING FACT Peter O'Brien is married to Australian star Miranda Otto.

Tom **Ramsay**

APPEARED 1987 - 1988. 1991.

LAST APPEARED 1991 > Left to live with estranged daughter Moira.

PLAYED BY Gary Files

Angie **Rebecchi**

APPEARED 1995 - 1996. 2002. 2003. 2004.

LAST APPEARED 2004 > Left to be with Big Kev. Cameo appearance in 2005.

PLAYED BY Lesley Baker

INTERESTING FACT When Lesley Baker first left Neighbours, fans launched a "Bring Back Angie" campaign on website www.perfectblend.net. The character was reinstated.

Stonefish **Rebecchi**

APPEARED 1994. 1995 - 1996. 2003.

LAST APPEARED 2003 > Moved with Angie to be with Big Kev in Colac.

PLAYED BY Anthony Engleman

Toadfish **Rebecchi**

FIRST APPEARED 1995

LAST APPEARED Still present..

PLAYED BY Ryan Moloney

INTERESTING FACT Toadie has an IQ of 135.

Tad **Reeves**

FIRST APPEARED 1998

LAST APPEARED 2002 > Moved to America to follow his passion in extreme sports.

PLAYED BY Jonathon Dutton

Brenda **Riley**

FIRST APPEARED 1991

LAST APPEARED 1992 > Relocated to Malaysia.

PLAYED BY Genevieve Lemon

Andrew **Robinson**

FIRST APPEARED 1991

LAST APPEARED 1992 > Lives with his mother.

PLAYED BY Shannon Holmes

Beverley **Robinson**

FIRST APPEARED 1987

LAST APPEARED 1990 > Left with Ewan for Perth.

PLAYED BY Lisa Armytage; Shaunna O'Grady

INTERESTING FACT The second Beverley Robinson, Shaunna O'Grady, is married to regular *Neighbours* director Chris Adshead.

Charlene **Robinson**

FIRST APPEARED 1986

LAST APPEARED 1988 > Went to live in Brisbane.

PLAYED BY Kylie Minogue

INTERESTING FACT Kylie Minogue, who during her time on *Neighbours* was dating her on-screen boyfriend Jason Donovan and sporting big hair and tight jeans, went on to become one of the world's biggest fashion and musical icons.

Gail **Robinson**

FIRST APPEARED 1987

LAST APPEARED 1989 > Left Paul to live in Tasmania with the man of her dreams. Cameo appearance in 2005.

PLAYED BY Fiona Corke

INTERESTING FACT Fiona Corke was exclusively dressed by Kamizole in each episode.

Hilary **Robinson**

FIRST APPEARED 1987

LAST APPEARED 1990 > Now works in a library. Cameo appearance in 2005.

PLAYED BY Anne Scott Pendlebury

Jim **Robinson**

FIRST APPEARED 1985

LAST APPEARED 1993 > Died of a heart attack.

PLAYED BY Alan Dale

INTERESTING FACT Now stars in popular American soap, *The OC*.

Lucy **Robinson**

FIRST APPEARED 1985

LAST APPEARED 1995. Cameo appearance in 2005.

PLAYED BY Kylie Flinker; Sasha Close; Melissa Bell

INTERESTING FACT Melissa Bell also starred in *E Street* and recently appeared on *Celebrity Overhaul*.

Matt **Robinson**

FIRST APPEARED 1989

LAST APPEARED 1991 > Left to be with Hilary.

PLAYED BY Ashley Paske

Paul **Robinson**

APPEARED 1985 - 1993. 2004.

LAST APPEARED Still present..

PLAYED BY Stefan Dennis

INTERESTING FACT Stefan Dennis is only 11 years younger than Alan Dale, who played his father.

Scott **Robinson**

FIRST APPEARED 1985

LAST APPEARED 1989 > Moved to Brisbane to join Charlene.

PLAYED BY Darius Perkins; Jason Donovan

INTERESTING FACT Jason Donovan's father, Terence Donovan, played Doug Willis, and his half-sister, Stephanie McIntosh, plays Sky Mangel. During his on-screen romance with Kylie Minogue, the couple would neither confirm nor deny they were dating. They were.

Terry **Robinson**

FIRST APPEARED 1985

LAST APPEARED 1985 > Died in prison.

PLAYED BY Maxine Klibingaitis

INTERESTING FACT Terry Robinson is the only *Neighbours* character to commit suicide.

Tony **Romeo**

FIRST APPEARED 1987
LAST APPEARED 1988 > Returned home to Perth.
PLAYED BY Nick Carrafa
INTERESTING FACT Later played Peter Hannay, Sarah Beaumont's fiancé.

Joel **Samuels**

FIRST APPEARED 1998
LAST APPEARED 2002 > Got a job on a ship in Queensland.
PLAYED BY Daniel MacPherson
INTERESTING FACT Discovered when competing in a triathlon, Daniel MacPherson went on to play PC Cameron Tait in *The Bill*.

Felicity **Scully**

FIRST APPEARED 1999
LAST APPEARED 2002 > Left to work for Lassiters in New York. Cameo appearance in 2005.
PLAYED BY Holly Valance
INTERESTING FACT Holly Valance is related to late British comedian Benny Hill.

Jack **Scully**

APPEARED 2001. 2002-2004. 2005.
LAST APPEARED 2005. Left to move to the USA to be with Nina Tucker.
PLAYED BY Paul Pantano; Jay Bunyan
INTERESTING FACT Paul Pantano debuted as Jack, but when Jay Bunyan took over later, the photo of Paul Pantano remained in the Scully family photo on display in the background of shots for some time.

Joe **Scully**

FIRST APPEARED 1999
LAST APPEARED 2004 > Went to look after his father in Bendigo.
PLAYED BY Shane Connor
INTERESTING FACT Shane Connor originally appeared on *Neighbours* as Phil Hoffman in 1991.

Lyn **Scully**

FIRST APPEARED 1999
LAST APPEARED Still present.
PLAYED BY Janet Andrewartha

Michelle **Scully**

APPEARED 1999 - 2003. 2004.
LAST APPEARED 2004 > Valda paid for Michelle to go to New York for her career.
PLAYED BY Kate Keltie

Oscar **Scully**

FIRST APPEARED 2003

LAST APPEARED Still present.

PLAYED BY Ingo Dammer-Smith

INTERESTING FACT Oscar Scully may be the first baby on television to be addicted to soap operas.

Susan **Smith**

FIRST APPEARED 1994

LAST APPEARED Still present.

PLAYED BY Jackie Woodburne

INTERESTING FACT Played Alan Fletcher's sister in *Cop Shop* and his wife in *Neighbours*.

Brett **Stark**

FIRST APPEARED 1993

LAST APPEARED 1996 > Left his mother to go sailing around the world. Cameo appearance in 2005.

PLAYED BY Brett Blewitt

Cheryl **Stark**

FIRST APPEARED 1993

LAST APPEARED 1996 > Died when hit by a car, saving Louise from the same fate.

PLAYED BY Caroline Gillmer; Colette Mann

INTERESTING FACT A pilot for a spin-off series surrounding the character of Cheryl was created, called *In Cheryl's Arms*. It never went to series.

Danni **Stark**

FIRST APPEARED 1993

LAST APPEARED 1996 > Left to work in fashion in Malaysia. Cameo appearance in 2005.

PLAYED BY Eliza Szonert

Darren **Stark**

APPEARED 1993. 1996 - 1998. 2004.

LAST APPEARED 2004 > Moved to Shepparton. Later joined by Libby and Ben. Cameo appearance in 2005.

PLAYED BY Scott Major; Todd MacDonald

Bree **Timmins**

FIRST APPEARED 2005
LAST APPEARED Still present.
PLAYED BY Sianoa Smit-McPhee

Dylan **Timmins**

FIRST APPEARED 2005
LAST APPEARED Still present.
PLAYED BY Damien Bodie
INTERESTING FACT Damien Bodie stars in Australian feature film *Hating Alison Ashley*, with ex-*Neighbours* star Delta Goodrem.

Janae **Timmins**

FIRST APPEARED 2005
LAST APPEARED Still present.
PLAYED BY Eliza Taylor-Cotter

Janelle **Timmins**

FIRST APPEARED 2005
LAST APPEARED Still present.
PLAYED BY Nell Feeney

Stingray **Timmins**

FIRST APPEARED 2004
LAST APPEARED Still present.
PLAYED BY Ben Nicholas

Nina **Tucker**

APPEARED 2002. 2003
LAST APPEARED 2004 > Left to be a star. Cameo appearance in 2005.
PLAYED BY Delta Goodrem
INTERESTING FACT Delta Goodrem's single, *Born to Try*, was written into her role as Nina Tucker on *Neighbours*. It went to number 1 and launched her successful music career. She played the title role in *Hating Alison Ashley*.

Darcy **Tyler**

APPEARED 2000-2003. 2004.2005.
LAST APPEARED 2005> After being hospitalised by Izzy, he appeared again in 2005.
PLAYED BY Mark Raffety

Sally **Upton**

FIRST APPEARED 1998
LAST APPEARED 1999 > Left after breaking up with Joel.
PLAYED BY Sally Davis

Sindi **Watts**

APPEARED 2002. 2003. 2004
LAST APPEARED Still present.
PLAYED BY Marisa Warrington

Sally **Wells**

FIRST APPEARED 1987
LAST APPEARED 1988 > Malcolm gave her a ticket to travel Europe with Eileen.
PLAYED BY Rowena Mohr

Anne **Wilkinson**

FIRST APPEARED 1996
LAST APPEARED 2000 > Got a transfer to Dawber University in Queensland to be with Billy.
PLAYED BY Brooke Satchwell
INTERESTING FACT Brooke Satchwell worked part time in a morgue before becoming an actress.

Lance **Wilkinson**

FIRST APPEARED 1995
LAST APPEARED 2001 > Left with Allana to a science fiction conference in America. Reappeared in 2005.
PLAYED BY Andrew Bibby

Ruth **Wilkinson**

FIRST APPEARED 1996
LAST APPEARED 1999 > Moved with the Martins. Cameo appearance in 2005.
PLAYED BY Ailsa Piper

Adam **Willis**

FIRST APPEARED 1990
LAST APPEARED 1991 > Transferred to finish his medical degree in Newcastle with Gemma. They married and settled there.
PLAYED BY Ian Williams

Brad **Willis**

FIRST APPEARED 1991

LAST APPEARED 1993 > Married Beth and left for Perth.

PLAYED BY Benjamin Mitchell; Scott Michaelson

INTERESTING FACT Benjamin Mitchell appeared as Brad Willis briefly and went on to play Cameron Hudson, Brad's rival.

Cody **Willis**

APPEARED 1989 - 1991. 1993 - 1996.

LAST APPEARED 1996 > Shot by a drug dealer in a shoot-out in Ramsay Street.

PLAYED BY Amelia Frid, Peta Brady

INTERESTING FACT Peta Brady has appeared since in Australian feature film *The Nugget* and in several episodes of *Kath and Kim*, playing Kelly.

Doug **Willis**

FIRST APPEARED 1990

LAST APPEARED 1994 > Became a building contractor at Darwin's Lassiters. Reappeared in 2005.

PLAYED BY Terence Donovan

INTERESTING FACT Terence Donovan (Doug Willis) is Jason Donovan's (Scott Robinson's) father in real life.

Gaby **Willis**

FIRST APPEARED 1991

LAST APPEARED 1994 > Left with Jack and Zac for Darwin, where Gaby took on the job of managing the Darwin Lassiter's and Outback Artists Tours. Cameo appearance in 2005.

PLAYED BY Rachel Blakely

Pam **Willis**

FIRST APPEARED 1990 - 1994. 1996

LAST APPEARED 1996 > Moved to live in Darwin with Doug and Gaby.

PLAYED BY Sue Jones

Zac **Willis**

FIRST APPEARED 1994

LAST APPEARED 1994 > Left with Gaby and Jack for Darwin.

PLAYED BY Jay Callahan

Mike **Young**

FIRST APPEARED 1986

LAST APPEARED 1990 > Went to look after his mother after she was in a car crash in Perth.

PLAYED BY Guy Pearce

INTERESTING FACT Guy Pearce started on *Neighbours* just two days after his final high school exams. After leaving, he starred in many Hollywood films.

FAR LEFT: Cast and crew celebrate the 3000th episode.
LEFT: The 1989 cast photo.
BELOW: The 10-year celebration in 1995.

The filming of the 20th anniversary special, shot in early 2005.

Cast 2005

Harold Bishop
Ian Smith

David Bishop
Kevin Harrington

Liljana Bishop
Marcella Russo

Serena Bishop
Lara Sacher

Lou Carpenter
Tom Oliver

Boyd Hoyland
Kyal Marsh

Izzy Hoyland
Natalie Bassingthwaighte

Max Hoyland
Stephen Lovatt

Stephanie Hoyland
Carla Bonner

Summer Hoyland
Marisa Siketa

Karl Kennedy
Alan Fletcher

Sky Mangel
Stephanie McIntosh

Connor O'Neill
Patrick Harvey

Stuart Parker
Blair McDonough

Toadfish Rebecchi
Ryan Moloney

Paul Robinson
Stefan Denis

Jack Scully
Jay Bunyan

Lyn Scully
Janet Andrewartha

Oscar Scully
Ingo Dammer-Smith

Susan Smith
Jackie Woodburne

Bree Timmins
Sianoa Smit-McPhee

Dylan Timmins
Damien Bodie

Scott Timmins
Ben Nicholas

Janelle Timmins
Nell Feeney

Janae Timmins
Eliza Taylor-Cotter

Sindi Watts
Marisa Warrington

Picture Credits

More Than a Serial

All photographs in this chapter are courtesy of Network Ten archives, Grundy archives or the HWT library.

A Star of a Show

All photographs in this chapter are courtesy of Network Ten archives, Grundy archives or the HWT library except where otherwise indicated.

P.20 GROUP WITH IAN SMITH. Erin Slattery.
P.20 PANORAMIC. Peter Bryant.
P.22 BUS. Erin Slattery.
P.22 SIGN. Erin Slattery.
P.22 BAND. Erin Slattery.
WEBSITE. Courtesy of bbc.co.uk/neighbours

20 Classic Characters

All photographs in this chapter are courtesy of Network Ten archives, Grundy archives or the HWT library except where otherwise indicated.

P.57. KYM VALENTINE (INSET). Peter Bryant.

Hunks, Babes and Romance

All photographs in this chapter are courtesy of Network Ten archives, Grundy archives or the HWT library.

Never a Dull Moment

All photographs in this chapter are courtesy of Network Ten archives, Grundy archives or the HWT library.

Lucky, Lucky, Lucky

All photographs in this chapter are courtesy of Network Ten archives, Grundy archives or the HWT library.

Four Months in the Making

All photographs in this chapter are courtesy of Network Ten archives, Grundy archives or the HWT library except where otherwise indicated.

P.104 TOM OLIVER ON SET. Erin Slattery.
P.108 FIRE. Peter Bryant.
P.109 BOARD. Erin Slattery.
P.109 PRODUCERS. Erin Slattery.
P.110 DESIGNER. Erin Slattery.
P.111 MAKEUP. Erin Slattery.
P.111 BOXING. Peter Bryant.
P.111 WARDROBE. Erin Slattery.
P.112 ACTORS ON SET. Peter Bryant.
P.114 PETER DODDS. Erin Slattery.
P.114 LOCATIONS. Erin Slattery.
P.116 UMBRELLAS. Peter Bryant.
P.116 KYM VALENTINE AND BLAIR MCDONOUGH. Peter Bryant.
P.116 NIGHT SHOOT. Peter Bryant.
P.116 WATER SHOOT. Peter Bryant.
P.116 NIGHT CARAVAN. Peter Bryant.
P.116 MICHELLE ANG. Peter Bryant.
P.116 CREW. Erin Slattery.
P.116 BOOM SHOT. Peter Bryant.
P.122 SUE WASHINGTON. Erin Slattery.

An A-Z of Neighbours

P.124 MEMORABILIA. Mark Taylor.
P.130 LASSITERS. Peter Bryant.
P.137 MEMORABILIA. Mark Taylor.

Brighter Lights

All photographs in this chapter are courtesy of Network Ten archives, Grundy archives or the HWT library.

Street Party

All photographs in this chapter are courtesy of Network Ten archives, Grundy archives or the HWT library except where otherwise indicated.

P.156 NEIGHBOURS FANS. Erin Slattery.
P.157 BUS DRIVER. Erin Slattery.
P.158 LINE TO PUB. Erin Slattery.
P.159 FAN. Erin Slattery.
P.159 HAROLD FANS. Erin Slattery.
P.160 CROWD. Erin Slattery.
P.160 NATALIE BASSINGTHWAIGHTE. Erin Slattery.
P.161 KARL FANS. Erin Slattery.
P.162 FANS CAMERA. Erin Slattery.
P.163 BUS GIRL. Erin Slattery.
P.163 MAX AND FAN. Erin Slattery.
P.163 PHOTO. Erin Slattery.
P.164 PETER DODDS. Erin Slattery.
P.164 FANS SIGN. Erin Slattery.
P.164 HOUSE. Erin Slattery.
P.164 BUS DRIVER. Erin Slattery.
P.164 PANORAMIC. Peter Bryant.
P.166 KIDS SIGN. Erin Slattery.
P.168 FANS PHOTOGRAPH. Erin Slattery
P.169 BUS. Erin Slattery.
P.169 BUS AT GATE. Erin Slattery.
P.172 PUB QUEUE. Erin Slattery.
P.172 INSIDE BUS. Erin Slattery
P.173 HAROLD. Erin Slattery.

The Full Story

All photographs in this chapter are courtesy of Network Ten archives, Grundy archives or the HWT library except where otherwise indicated.

P.177 MEMORABILIA. Mark Taylor.
P.179 MEMORABILIA. Mark Taylor.
P.181 MEMORABILIA. Mark Taylor.
P.183 MEMORABILIA. Mark Taylor.
P.187 MEMORABILIA. Mark Taylor.
P.191 4000TH BIRTHDAY SHOT. Peter Bryant.
P.194 CAST AND CREW SHOT. Peter Bryant.
P.195 CAST AND CREW SHOT (10). Peter Bryant.

Complete Character List

All photographs in this chapter are courtesy of Network Ten archives, Grundy archives or the HWT library.